THE EVERYDAY WRITING CENTER

THE EVERYDAY WRITING CENTER

A Community of Practice

ANNE ELLEN GELLER
MICHELE EODICE
FRANKIE CONDON
MEG CARROLL
ELIZABETH H. BOQUET

2007
UTAH STATE UNIVERSITY PRESS
Logan, Utah

Utah State University Press
Logan, Utah 84322–7800

Manufactured in the United States of America
Cover design by Barbara Yale-Read
Cover art "Trickster's Morning Song," by Judith Kalina. Website: www.judithkalina.com

Library of Congress Cataloging-in-Publication Data

The everyday writing center : a community of practice / Anne Ellen Geller ... [et al.].
    p. cm.
  Includes bibliographical references and index.
  ISBN 978-0-87421-656-1 (pbk. : alk. paper)
  1. Writing centers. 2. English language–Rhetoric–Study and teaching. 3. Interdisciplinary approach
in education. I. Geller,
Anne Ellen, 1969-
  PE1404.G385 2007
  808'.0420711–dc22

                    2006036669

CONTENTS

PREFACE

This book has its origins, as many academic books do, in conversations over dinner and drinks at conferences, WCenter listserv back-chatter over email, and informal exchanges about the intrigues and curiosities of the everyday in our writing centers and institutions. The five of us represent writing center directors at small, medium, and large colleges and universities, private and public, religiously-affiliated and secular, and we sought opportunities to speak across our different institutional missions, goals, student populations, and resources. Soon we found ourselves looking for common projects that offered some potential for generalizability across writing centers and that actively worked against the meme of the highly contextualized, "localized" writing center. And, though a book with five co-authors seemed initially like the kind of idea that only makes sense late on a Saturday night at a conference hotel bar, we received enough encouragement from one another, and from a certain cigar-smoking, bourbon-breathed editor, to think that maybe we should give it a whirl. Rather than turn to writing individual chapters for an edited collection, we were determined to work through a series of ideas we thought essential to writing center work and to present those ideas in a form that enacted the principles we espouse: a five way collaboration on every aspect of the text.

Across our differences, as the web of friendships that compose the "we" of our book began to flourish, we discovered in each other some common ground that became clear and very dear to each of us. Beyond listening to each other deeply, we each, in listening, still the impulse to do, to fix, to solve. We tend instead to turn away, reflectively, from the urge to resolve one another's problems or to advise courses of action, to discount the complexity of one another's stories. Each of us tries to experience our discoveries of everyday problems, absences, gaps, and needs not as moments of crisis that must be resolved quickly, but as opportunities rich with possibility. These occasions pique our curiosity, our sense of wonderment, and our predilection toward creative, intellectual engagement . . . or mischief.

In some sense, this book is composed of those quotidian moments. As often as not, when we try to talk about the writing of this book, we wind up talking about where we were, what the weather was like, what we ate. To jog each other's memories, we say, "You remember. Frankie was taking the notes, sitting at the kitchen table in her Clifford the Big Red Dog

pajamas and Michele kept asking Anne, 'How do you want your eggs?'"
Or "I don't remember that conversation. That must have been when you
two were out smoking on the deck in the freezing cold!" We came to
know each other's needs and preferences—who takes a little afternoon
nap, who can't do hazelnut coffee—as we came to know each other's
particular commitments to ideas. In deciding to work *with* each other,
we tacitly agreed to work *for* each other, as Day and Eodice describe this
"completion of care" in their book *(First Person)2: A Study of Co-Authoring
in the Academy*. In part, this desire grew out of the seriousness with which
we take and have taken one another's intellectual and creative abilities,
political convictions and activism, and one another's ideas, perspectives,
and experiences. We discovered new ways to conceptualize the everyday
writing center, drawing on Wenger's *community of practice* and the idea
of a *learning culture*. And, as happens in communities of practice and in
learning cultures, the ideas and concerns that may have once belonged
to or originated with one of us became collective matters or moments of
possibility. In the fullness of time, and through friendship that has been
both personal and professional, we have chosen to learn from and adapt
to one another's ideas, discovering the ways in which our individual perceptions speak to, inform, enrich, and deepen in the minds of others.

Cultivating communities of practice and learning cultures is never
seamless, neat, or easy. Representing those to readers is almost as challenging. Early in the process, we decided to highlight our collaborative
over our individual contributions. Some of our discarded attempts
were playful—capitalizing "We," for example, whenever we spoke with
an authorial voice, or crafting anagrams that would put a name to our
Frankenstein, using the first few letters of our first names—Micbeth
Frannemeg—or only the letters of our last names: Aunt D.Q. Bricolage.
Like Ede and Lunsford, who considered Annalisa Edesford to represent
them both, or Myka Vielstimmig, the hybrid persona created by coau-
thors Kathleen Blake Yancey and Michael Spooner, we longed to press
ourselves, our very names, together to demonstrate how much melding
our minds meant to us.[1] In this final version, our decision seems conventional by comparison. Our names are listed in reverse alphabetical
order for no reason other than that someone suggested it and it seemed
as good a solution as anything. In the text itself, we use "we" even when
representing what are clearly individual experiences (experiences, in
other words, that obviously occurred in only one of our five centers).
In this way, we hope to highlight the fact that, though an event may
have been brought to bear on the conversation by one or the other of

us, we have worked collectively to understand the significance of the moment. When you read, we hope you will hear our collective voice. More than that, we invite you into that collective. Just as we occasionally said to each other "I don't think it's that simple" or "hey, you missed a spot," so too you may wish to offer a "yes, and" or a "yeah, but" or a "not quite." At these moments, we hope you sense in the air our "we" as a whiff of inclusion, an invitation. We hope to put you in dialogue with us. This requires considering your own personal awareness, practice, and inquiry. As you enter into dialogues with this book, you enter into discussions with yourself as well as with us.[2] And as you place yourself along the same continua on which we have found ourselves—sometimes more invested, sometimes less; sometimes more knowledgeable, sometimes less—you will be moving through and among the communities of practice of which you are already a part. Or maybe you will find yourself, as we have, seeking new ones.

Our unified voice dignifies the mess of learning—the worries all of us have felt and shared about whether we belong, the value of our contributions in both personal and professional terms, the points of disagreement and of contestation. Yet we still long to celebrate and show off the hard work required for sustained learning over distance, time, and difference.

Finally, in writing a preface about ourselves as co-authors, we wish to challenge the tendency of academic readers to think of knowledge production and the written text as individual labor and property. You may, as you read, attempt to parse out our individual contributions (but be warned—there are passages that now we are unable to identify with one or the other of us). But we hope that our "we" will stand in as our "why?" in response to those efforts to parse, and will serve as a reminder of those longstanding assumptions about authorship in the academy that may unwittingly undermine the most sincere efforts to learn with others.

ACKNOWLEDGMENTS

Many people have supported us as we ate, drank, sang, and talked our way through this book. We begin by thanking Michael Spooner, without whom we would not have even thought about, much less accomplished, writing this book together in one voice. We thank David Carroll and Kami Day, who endured our occupation of kitchen tables and every other nook and cranny of their homes, with characteristic generosity and good cheer.

The International Writing Centers Association supported us with a travel grant that funded conversations crucial to the early drafts of this project, and several colleagues in the IWCA deserve special mention: Neal Lerner, Harry Denny, Ben Rafoth, Melissa Ianetta, Lauren Fitzgerald, and Jeanne Simpson. We also acknowledge participants in Summer Institutes 2004, 2005, and 2006, who kept us grounded in the everyday experiences of writing centers beyond our own.

Our colleges and universities respectively support our research in more ways than we could possibly enumerate, so we extend our gratitude to the members of the Clark University, University of Kansas, St. Cloud State University, Rhode Island College, Fairfield University, and University of Oklahoma communities. When we are unable to talk with each other, we are fortunate to have many model teacher-researchers on our own campuses, with whom we can share ideas, frustrations, and successes. We have appreciated feedback and support from Kathy Nantz, Mariann Regan, Bob Epstein, John Thiel, Richard Regan, Betsy Bowen, Kirk Branch, Mary Catherine Davidson, Moira Ozias, Gino DiIorio, Lea Graham, Cheryl Turner Elwell, Marjorie Roemer, Jenn Cook, Randy DeSimone, Claudine Griggs, Jennifer Mitchell, Tracy Ore, Catherine Fox and the Community Anti-Racism Education (CARE) Leadership Team at SCSU.

We are also tremendously grateful to our students, both tutors and writers, who challenge our most cherished beliefs at every turn.

We especially thank those anonymous peer reviewers—later revealed to be Laurie Grobman, Harvey Kail, and Elisabeth Piedmont-Marton—who provided valuable insight and direction during revision stages of the manuscript.

Finally, we are able to enter into this work with openness, love, and wicked senses of humor because we have such shining examples of those qualities in our lives outside the writing center: For this, a big shout out goes to the folks at the horse barn. And we thank our families—especially Dan, Lucy, and Grace, Dawn, Kim, and Meredith, Dan Bedeker, Kami Day, David Carroll, Michael Condon, Pat Boquet, Bert Boquet (the first and the second), Cristina Parsons—and our dearest friends.

1

INTRODUCTION

And I forgot the element of chance introduced by circumstances, calm or
haste, sun or cold, dawn or dusk, the taste of strawberries or abandon-
ment, the half-understood message, the front page of newspapers, the
voice on the telephone, the most anodyne conversation, the most anony-
mous man or woman, everything that speaks, makes noise, passes by,
touches us lightly, meets us head on.

Jacques Sojcher, qtd in de Certeau, xvi

Walk through a morning with us—we're out the door, heading to campus, strolling into the building, pulling out the office keys, and flipping
on the lights. You know, the routine: turn on the computer, take off the
coat, get to work. The voice mail message light blinks "Good Morning"
in its own Morse code; the computer sings as it powers up, dinging one,
two, twenty-five new email messages received. The clock continues its
steady march toward the first class, and payroll must receive an accurate
accounting of tutors' hours by noon today if checks are to appear in
their boxes on Friday. These kinds of needs, and dozens more, demand
our attention every hour. Yet it is all too easy to leave the writing center
at the end of the day feeling complacent, believing that preparing a
payroll, stepping in for a sick tutor, or even planning an upcoming staff
meeting comprises the extent of our writing center's work. As necessary
as these tasks are, we might be so consumed by them that we miss something else: the most interesting moments in our workday have probably
not demanded our attention at all. As we shut off the lights and turn
the key in the lock once more, we should wonder about the significance of all that we could have noticed in our everyday spaces: the role
reversal of two of the writing center's prized action figures, Pokey and
Shakespeare—Will, on this day, uncharacteristically, giving Pokey a ride.
Pokey's skinny orange front legs are perched on the Bard's shoulders—a
real switch in human-horse relations, a quiet surprise. Who did it, and
why? The culprit, when finally identified, simply replies, "Equality." Or
the scene composed of a bright red cardinal puppet, an all-too-realis-
tic gun, and the Western literature anthology. Some kind of threat? A
weapon waiting to be retrieved later? No, a "tableau," set up by one of
the tutors, called "shooting the canon."

Our attention is constantly split between moments like these and the larger, louder issues that relentlessly nip at us, demanding our attention and response. In the face of institutional deadlines, we are tempted to relegate such moments to the backburner, to assume they are beneath consideration, amusing but not pressing. In our haste, we may fail to consider the ways these moments hint at the degree to which our tutors[1] feel invested in the work of the writing center, the connections our tutors are making to their intellectual interests and to their lives outside the center. We may not capitalize, in other words, on the ability of everyday exchanges to tell us something about our writing centers as representing what Etienne Wenger calls "communities of practice."[2] Perhaps we've lost our ability to slow down, notice, and consider most of the specific moments within the seemingly routine demands we are so often pressed to meet as directors. Arguing that our field has become "*trapped* in theory," Kurt Spellmeyer calls for us instead to turn to "an alternative so mundane that we have passed it over time after time in our scramble for sophistication and prestige. That alternative is ordinary sensuous life, which is not an 'effect' of how we think but the ground of thought itself" (893–894).

In conversation with each other, the five of us realized that we wanted more permission, from one another, from our staffs, from our colleagues within our institutions and within our field, to practice what Michel de Certeau calls "ways of dwelling" in uncomfortable places (30), to embrace situations in which we and our tutors have been thrust. We wanted to bring the smallest moments of our work, thought about deeply, together with our largest institutional and intellectual concerns. And we sought ways to support ourselves and our staffs as we began that work.

Wenger explains, "We all have our own theories and ways of understanding the world, and our communities of practice are places where we develop, negotiate, and share them" (48). Through these communities, participants develop a "shared repertoire" (82) of practice, exchanges where there exists no "dichotomy between the practical and the theoretical, ideals and reality, or talking and doing" (48). To understand Wenger is to understand that multiple communities of practice intersect in overlapping spheres in each person's life each day. By the time you arrive at work, you have already interacted with members of several of your own communities of practice (whether you would call them such or not). Morning negotiations with your family, helpful hints from a trainer at your gym, meeting with faculty to discuss the choices for next fall's first-year seminar book—all of these moments place you in relation to others with whom you share what Wenger describes as "the dynamics of everyday existence, improvisation, coordination, and interactional choreography" (13). If you are reading this book, you are part of yet another community of practice: writing centers. Writing centers, as communities of practice, have a history of exploring the ways in which meaning is negotiated among mutually engaged participants, negotiation that "in practice always involves the whole person" (47). If we accept this characterization of writing centers, set next to Wenger's ideas, then we have to consider a philosophy of writing center work which is designed for learning, and as Wenger claims, "designing for learning cannot be based on a division of labor between learners and nonlearners, between those who organize learning and those who realize it, or between those who create meaning and those who execute it" (234). In other words, this design must be based on something other than the familiar stratification between directors and tutors, tutors and writers, directors and professors, peer tutors and professional instructors. Though all of these participants come from their own many sites of practice, within the writing center they become members of the writing center community of practice and, as such, should be viewed as learners on common ground. Lest you think us naïve, we don't imagine we have succeeded in one paragraph in eliminating conflict, disagreement, competition, and disenfranchising hierarchical relations. Instead, we acknowledge that writing centers—like *all* communities of practice—are "neither a haven for togetherness nor an island of intimacy insulated from political and social relations" (77).

Writing center scholarship has long positioned writing centers as potentially insulated from these tensions—we often conceive of our spaces as safe houses, for example—and some fear the dissolution of community that might result from acknowledging tension; but avoiding this kind of work, according to Wenger, denies the potential of such tension—a tension that is dynamic, necessary and ever present. Although recent scholarship does address the tensions and challenges outlined above,[3] the goal of such acknowledgment should not be, according to Wenger, to rid ourselves of these challenges, which would be futile and unrealistic, but rather to embrace the idea that "[d]isagreement, challenges, and competition can all be forms of participation" (77).

We cannot and are not advocating that "disagreement, challenges, and competition" should thrive in all forms and at all costs. In fact, it has long been acknowledged by scholars in our field that in the context of traditional schooling, this trio of factors contributes to the potentially alienating effects of typical instruction. Despite all our talk about collaboration and community, we walk through our classes, through our buildings, through our campuses, through our neighborhoods, disconnected from what matters to us. If we attempt to ignore these negative influences on our work and on our students, we reify troubling institutional impulses in other ways: participating in or somehow supporting rote training, standardized tests, and obsessive bean-counting, for example. How does the writing center function as an institutional space that lets us step in and speak to those matters? Could what Nancy Grimm terms our "good intentions" be keeping students from building on their own cultural capital in safe and productive ways? What about school matters? How do we make one another matter?

We believe we matter because of what we do. Wenger reminds us that "communities of practice are about content—about learning as a living experience of negotiating meaning—not about form" (229). And not about (filling out) forms. We look to Ivan Illich, who claims, "Neither learning nor justice is promoted by schooling because educators insist on packaging instruction with certification" (11). As new staff education manuals land on our desks, as discussions of CRLA certification for tutors surface again and again and again on the WCenter listserv, we sense a move toward knowledge as containment, as commodity, and a move away from the genuine moments of collaboration that lead to knowledge-(re)creation. In some ways, this move toward certification simply reduces the complexity of tutoring, as de Certeau writes, to "the data that can most easily be grasped, recorded, transported, and examined in secure places" (20). Is it possibly true, as the author of *Leadership Jazz*, Max DePree, states, that "the health of an organization is inversely proportional to the size of the manual?"[4] We worry about the degree to which the neatly-packaged representation of our rich, multi-layered, everyday writing center lives becomes a set of "symbolic practices that substitute for action all too easily" (Spellmeyer 894), and fear that we may, as Spellmeyer warns, be close to accepting symbolic practices in place of "actions that can lead to meaningful change" (894). Wenger echoes this in noting that "whereas training aims to create an inbound trajectory targeted at competence in a specific practice, education must strive to open new dimensions for the negotiation of self" (263). We want to envision a writing center that is, as Anne Ruggles Gere describes in her work on the literacy practices of 19th century women's writing groups, "constructed by desire, by the aspirations and imaginations of its participants" ("Kitchen Tables and Rented Rooms" 80).

Rather than exchange pedagogical currency (a pre-fabricated script, for example, of a "model" tutoring session), our aim here is to articulate and elaborate the conditions under which writing center staff can be supported in their search to be in-the-moment-at-the-point-of-need knowledge producers in the writing center. In his book, *Critique of Everyday Life*, Henri Lefebvre writes:

> Where economy and philosophy meet lies the theory of fetishism. Money, currency, commodities, capital, are nothing more than relations between human beings (between "individual," qualitative, human tasks). And yet these relations take on the appearance and the form of *things* external to human beings. The appearance becomes the reality; because [people] believe that these "fetishes" exist outside of themselves they really do function like objective things. (178)

Throughout this book, we argue that we are guilty, in our writing centers as in our culture at large, of fetishizing the commodities—like time, normalized practices, identifiable policies—rather than focusing on the interactions between and among these categories. In contrast, we see the pedagogy for which we advocate as praxis compellingly situated in the relational—not as things, but as ways of acting with and for one another. We see the ways of knowing of which we speak as a gift to be passed on and passed around rather than as a form of currency to be exchanged.

In his book *The Gift: Imagination and the Erotic Life of Property*, Lewis Hyde writes that "in a group that derives its cohesion from a circulation of gifts, the conversion of gifts to commodities will have the effect of fragmenting the group, or even destroying it" (75). We seek in this book not to codify and prescribe, not to commodify what we have done and continue to do singly and together (a practice that we believe would reproduce the conditions of fragmentation and alienation Hyde warns us of), but perhaps to teach and "learn by faint clues and indirections" (Whitman in Hyde 280) and hence to "widen out the boundaries of our being" (Neruda in Hyde 281). We see ourselves united with one another and with the writing center community, not by virtue of shared mastery of a body of concretized practices, but rather by virtue of shared gifts.

This book is concerned with the betwixt-and-between state in which so much of our work must be done. As such, within and among chapters, readers will find theoretical explorations woven into descriptions of life on the ground in the writing center, as we make an effort to use the *hows* to illuminate the whys and the *whys* to illuminate the hows.

We ask you to think with us about what it might mean to revel in the in-between of everyday writing center occasions, to experience the time pressures of our days differently, to give tutors ways to truly inhabit the intellectual as well as the physical space of the center, to help them bring their most creative selves to the table during each conference, and to address issues of race and racism on our campuses. Rather than seeking agreement and rote responses, tutors can risk anarchy and opt for ebullience, as Ivan Illich observes (36). How do we make these conditions possible in our writing centers? For us, attention first to the everydayness of our work can uncover our communities of practice and make way for a learning culture to emerge. For example, our tutors wait for us to uncover their "messages" (why is Pokey riding Shakespeare?) and to use them as openings for shared laughter as well as for extended conversation about the details of their lives inside and outside the writing center. We in turn have to pay attention, in these cases and in countless others in the days, weeks, months of our writing centers' operations, to the not-quite-said, to the lived moments in the writing center and what they are telling us. By noticing these moments, we signal to our tutors that we are indeed present with them, attending to the subtleties of their writing center days. In our everyday lives in the writing center, moments like those we've cited above, the dozens to follow in this book, and the scores that had to be left out, remind us to keep both uncertainty and opportunity possible at all times.

LEADERS IN A LEARNING CULTURE

Parker Palmer writes in *The Courage to Teach* (1998) that:

> Community does not emerge spontaneously from some relational reflex, especially not in the complex and often conflicted institutions where most teachers work. If we are to have communities of discourse about teaching and learning—communities that are intentional about the topics to be pursued and the ground rules to be practiced—we need leaders who can call people toward that vision. (156)

Some aspect of this book hinges on the questions of what kind of leadership is possible and desirable in a writing center and what kind of leaderful learning can take place in and around a writing center. In *The Learning Paradigm College* (2003), John Tagg describes two kinds of leadership: structural and functional. Structural leaders, Tagg writes, have a leadership role by virtue of their position within an institution (deans, for example, or provosts or presidents). In relation to our tutors, to the student-writers who visit our writing centers, and to faculty who note and value our expertise, we directors occupy this role. Tagg also describes, however, functional leaders—those who assume a leadership role out of a sense of mission, of need, of purpose and who require the participation of others to accomplish this purpose (338). Tagg explains that structural leaders are often expected to deal only with the maintenance of things as they are—the preservation and success of the status quo (339). In order for leaders in the post-secondary context to instigate, promote, and effectively sustain institutional transformation, Tagg writes that structural leaders must also be functional leaders who "will use the authority of their offices to achieve the mission of institutional transformation" (339). He proposes that we move beyond maintenance mode, beyond filling the squares on the organizational chart, and embrace the mantle of institutional leader as well.

Many of us have, to one degree or another, the sense of mission and purpose that Tagg describes. We have lacked, however, the conviction that we have enough (or any) structural authority to lead our institutions in the work. The demands of things-as-they-are have seemed so constraining that we have felt it necessary to prepare our tutors and writers to live, work, and write in the world-as-is. Recognizing that meaningful change is next to impossible to see, we press on and embrace a kind of pessimistic pragmatism. Still, with all of this, we want to, need to, cling to "idealism."[5] Tagg and other theorists of organizational change argue that in order to see a world of possibility, we need to see what *is*, not as normal, given, and permanent, but as strange, provisional, and mutable. Further, Tagg suggests that our effectiveness depends upon our willingness and our ability to recognize the institutional authority we do have and to claim the functional authority to call one another, our tutors and students, and our institutions to a sense of mission, of purpose.

The five of us support each other when we feel dissatisfied with givens, rules, platitudes, tropes, maxims that seem to have come unmoored from any deep reasoning that might have produced them to begin with. We remind each other to be curious: We tend to read widely and to find points and patterns of intersection across disciplines. We encourage each other not to feel bound by what has been written precisely about writing centers or about composition and rhetoric, and we have found meaning and value for our writing center work in architecture, music, poetry, social theory, organizational theory, quantum theory, critical race theory, and much more. Finally, we prompt each other to be driven by a sense of purpose that extends beyond what might be traditionally thought of as the boundaries of writing center work. We have individually and collectively tended to resist any suggestion that we can do this much and no more.

CHAPTER PREVIEWS

In the first chapter, "Trickster at Your Table," we discuss trickster figures who teach us a habit of mind that helps us notice and revel in the accidental, the unforeseen, the surprise. We don't mean to suggest, though, that directors should focus on producing trickster tutors. What we think is important is encouraging a community of practice that allows for change, mutability, learning. We recognize that, although learning can be facilitated, as Wenger argues, it "cannot be designed. Ultimately, it belongs to the realm of experience and practice. It follows the negotiation of meaning; it moves on its own terms. It slips through the cracks; it creates its own cracks. Learning happens, design or no design" (Wenger 225). For this reason, in this book and in our work in our writing centers and at our respective institutions, we resist prescribing traveling practices. There is no syllabus here, no textbook; in fact, we warn against the over-reliance on textbooks which can reify memes and mental models—those models which contain rather than expand practices. As Peter Senge describes this problem, "new insights fail to get put into practice because they conflict with deeply held internal images of how the world works, images that limit us to familiar ways of thinking and acting" (*The Fifth Discipline* 174).

Rather, we look at the model of trickster in conjunction with Wenger's communities of practice as a way to recognize in the daily moments of each of our writing centers and classrooms the grounding of our individual learning communities. These moments help us to foster tutors and writers as participants in those communities, participants who are able to negotiate meaning, to cross boundaries—an ability that can only be achieved when "participants are able to recognize an experience of meaning in each other and to develop enough of a shared sense of competence to do some mutual learning" (140). As beings that expose contradictions and question received ideas, tricksters provide a window into the writing center's role in re-inscribing social and cultural norms on campus as well.

Next we address the perennial lament of writing center workers (and indeed, people) everywhere: the issue of time. In "Beat (Not) the (Poor) Clock," we acknowledge the crushing weight of the second hand as it sweeps past in our sessions and in our lives. Successfully balancing our desire and need—(or perceived need) to respond quickly—to students, to our tutors, to our institutions, to our world—with our yearning for slow, satisfying reflection requires making time an explicit focus of our work. So we explore the opportunities we have in writing centers for manipulating our experiences of time, downplaying Total Quality Management models for education and highlighting time's elastic properties instead. In addition, leading functionally and contributing to learning cultures require long, future-oriented views of our work and the constant conviction that past, present and future always inform one another.

Next, we turn to the heart of the writing center, the tutors as learners and writers. Through both chapters "Origami, Anyone?: Tutors as Learners" and "Straighten Up and Fly Right: Writers as Tutors, Tutors as Writers," we are more concerned about what our tutors can *learn* and *imagine* than we are about what they *know* (In fact, we're also more concerned with our own ability to continually learn and imagine than we are with what we already know as directors.). Once time opens up, other opportunities arise, as well as occasions to remember what keeps tutors—and us—in a mindset of exploration with one and other and the world around us. These two chapters look closely at these issues and how communities of practice might be fostered not only in formal staff education courses, but in everyday interactions among tutors, writers, and directors. Specifically, we look at:

- renewing directors' and tutors' experience of what Sheryl Fontaine calls "the beginner's mind"
- fostering reflective practice
- creating a shared repertoire
- encouraging tutors to be boundary workers
- promoting shared ownership and negotiation of meaning

We hope that readers will see ways to create more collaborative writing center communities where "what [tutors] learn is not a static subject matter but the very process of being engaged in, and participating in developing, an ongoing practice" (Wenger 95).

In "Everyday Racism: Anti-Racism Work and Writing Center Practice," we explore our own commitments to diversity on our campuses by looking through the lenses of our own centers. As a field, we have spun a writing center narrative so universal that we don't need to think about certain matters (like identity, racism, and disenfranchisement) in the context of writing centers because our founding principles are so inherently inclusive—or so we think. Periodically, and with a regularity that signals rhythm, pace, and pattern to us, our claims to *community* in and through our writing centers ring hollow. We are awakened from a drowsy comfort with things-as-they-are by a flash of insight, the sudden realization that the world with its catastrophes of inequality, domination, control, consent, and the ceding of authority is inside our writing center . . . not kept safely at bay as we had imagined. We realize that we have failed to account for the operations of power, of identity, and of meaning-making in our centers. As Wenger reminds us, there can be no community without diversity. Further, counter-hegemonic voices within communities of practice signal a greater investment in that community than do the voices of acquiescence (77).

This chapter asks what our work would look like if we used our strengths—the strengths associated with writing center work—to transform our centers and our institutions. Drawing on critical theories of race and racial formation, we consider how and why our centers might both be implicated in perpetuating institutional racism and also become potential sites for meaningful transformation.

The final chapter, "Everyday Administration, or Are We Having Fun Yet?" addresses our work within and beyond the physical boundaries of our centers. In this chapter, we consider the complexities and joys not just of managing, but of leading. We propose structures and conditions that allow tutors, students, our colleagues and our institutions to do their best work and their deepest learning. We hope that the ways we perform as administrators on our campuses would be consonant with the ways we work in our centers, and we argue for a philosophy of writing center administration that resists compartmentalization and certainty and strives for congruence and collaboration.

This chapter, for us, culminates (for the purposes of this book) our search for constancy among our philosophies, our senses of mission and purpose in our writing center work and the ways in which we engage beyond the boundaries of our centers in the work of institutional transformation. We urge an administrative philosophy and practice that clearly distinguish means from ends. To adapt an analogy pursued by John Tagg, we assert that to suggest that the chief mission of a writing center is to deliver tutoring in writing. is akin to suggesting that the chief mission of General Motors is to produce assembly lines (18). When we consider seriously the distinctions between means and ends, we can discern that at the heart of meaningful writing center administration lies not efficiency, marketing, and record-keeping (these are peripheral matters, in fact), but the leaderful, learningful stewardship of a dynamic learning and writing culture and community.

2

TRICKSTER AT YOUR TABLE

More conservative minds deprive coincidence of meaning by treating it
as background noise or garbage, but the shape-shifting mind pesters the
distinction between accident and essence and remakes this world out of
whatever happens.

Lewis Hyde

Walk with us now through another doorway, this time not into the physical space of the writing center, but into the mythical space of Trickster. Doorways represent, in fact, crossroads for Trickster figures, sites of contingency and leakage. Lewis Hyde writes, "All Tricksters like to hang around the doorway, that being one of the places where deep-change accidents occur" (124). We like to think of our writing centers as places where deep-change accidents occur, of the doorways to our writing centers as something other than the familiar gate-keeping devices; and we use this chapter to explore the application of the concept of Trickster to the work of the writing center and to the creation and support of learning communities within these sites.

WHO/WHAT IS TRICKSTER?

Common Trickster figures include familiar classical god-like characters such as Loki and Hermes, or the Raven, Blue Jay, and Fox; and, especially in North America, Coyote.[1] As the name suggests, Trickster loves to play tricks on other gods (and sometimes on humans and animals). But his main function is that of "boundary-crosser" (Hyde 7). Hyde in fact refers to Trickster as "the god of the threshold in all its forms" (7–8). Trickster crosses both physical and social boundaries; Trickster is often a traveler, and he frequently breaks societal rules, blurring connections and distinctions between "right and wrong, sacred and profane, clean and dirty, male and female, young and old, living and dead" (Hyde 7), changing shape (turning into an animal, for example) to move between worlds. The implications of Trickster stories are many, according to Michael Webster, professor of English at Grand Valley State University:

> [T]rickster stories . . . have something to say about how culture gets created, and about the nature of intelligence. Trickster represents a certain

flexibility of mind and spirit, a willingness to defy authority and invent clever solutions that keeps cultures (and stories) from becoming too stagnant. (http://faculty.gvsu.edu/websterm/Tricksters.htm)[2]

Trickster figures are impossible to package, manage, school, or concretize. In some ways, then, they personify chaos, the disorderly order inherent in all systems. As physicist James Gleick tells us in his book *Chaos*, "[T]he disorderly behavior of simple systems [acts] as a creative process. It [generates] complexity, richly organized patterns, sometimes stable, sometimes unstable, sometimes finite, sometimes infinite, but always with the fascination of living things" (43). So what are the implications for our work if we embrace a Trickster chaos and become more mindful of how the fascination of living things and ideas can change our practice? The chaos of Trickster moments may be funny or shocking. But as with any rupture of the assumed, they may also shove us headlong into learning anew what it means to work responsibly and in more principled ways in the context of the writing center.

We'd like to capture the movement, connections, risks, and coincidences that take place in staff education and in writing tutorials, and from them suggest ways to cultivate a Trickster mind, one that can be awakened to and can awaken moments of discernment about uncertainty. But our proposal is not another lesson plan or a workshop to teach tutors to be Tricksters, and we do not (and cannot) offer an easy prescription for recognizing Trickster; ours is a proposal to teach a mindfulness to Trickster and possibly a Trickster mind. We have been surprised at what has happened as we have identified Trickster moments in our own practices and in the practices of our staffs. And from our surprise, we have learned about ourselves and our writing centers.

We live in an either-or world, a world that doesn't offer much opportunity to be uncertain, or tickled, or puzzled. How much room do we leave, in our day-to-day existence, to be surprised, to try out different eyes, as Coyote, a common Trickster figure, does? In one tale, Coyote tosses his eyes up into the trees one too many times; now he can no longer enjoy the long view or retrieve his eyes. His blandishments bring him a mouse eye and a buffalo eye as replacements—but what he sees is definitely not the same. A new worldview, brought on by this uncomfortable fit, is Coyote's way of turning his foolishness into ours: "Coyote is said to trick the learner into the lesson, almost giving one the notion that things are not as they seem, until the lesson is done and the wisdom gained." [3]

We, our tutors, and our writers are tricked into lessons in our writing centers every day. Here's one example: Missy, one of the tutors, sits at a table in the writing center playing Scrabble with a student. They're laughing. What's going on? Where's the paper? Are they "off task"? How will we know if they venture too far "off task"? Should we interrupt? Leave Missy a "See me" note"? Depending on the paradigm for teaching and learning that operates in that writing center, the director's interpretations and reactions will vary.

In reality, the student in this scene is multilingual, wants to improve his English language vocabulary, and loves to play Scrabble. Trickster-like, Missy meets uncertainty ("What will people think if I'm playing a game with a student?" "Will the student be satisfied with a tutoring session disguised as a game of Scrabble?") and takes what might be described as an unconventional approach, one that isn't found in a training manual. Missy sets aside habit and repetition and instead invokes Augustine, who views play as "vital to the work of the gods," as a "divine [form] of subversion" (Babcock 10).

The Scrabble scene is interesting precisely because there is no accounting for a moment like this one in any standard tutoring advice or manual. We could imagine offering tutors such advice—"When working with students on linguistic fluency, play some word-games with them."—but Missy's decision implies so much more about peerness, about expertise, about rules, about environment. A line in a manual, by necessity, flattens out a scene that otherwise speaks volumes. Volumes, for example, about the philosophy of the writing center in which Missy works: a center in which tutors don't worry about being "off-task" with students; a center in which serious work with language doesn't always look or feel so serious; a center where "uncertainty creates freedom to discover meaning" and where "mindfully considering data not as stable commodities but as sources of ambiguity [leads people to] become more observant" (Langer 130, 133). Statement of the obvious on this page: Having a Scrabble board game available, then, means tutors and writers (or anyone) can play Scrabble together. The Scrabble game, in this instance, supports conditions that allow tutors to work in alternate ways with writers and indicates something about the center's assumptions about the ways time is spent.

Trickster moments like this one can be generative, can nudge us to be mindful, to notice more. They can move us to change. Of course, Trickster will arrive, invited or not; Trickster remains amoral, non-judgmental; Trickster does not insist he "teach us a lesson," yet we can learn from his actions. In order to do so, a certain readiness and mindset must precede the visit. Are we willing to be awakened by jarring moments, by anxieties about our practices, policies, and procedures? Are we prepared to question the value of a set of prescribed and relatively stable steps that get the tutor from here to there in exchange for a philosophy that might leave tutors and writers standing alone (yet together) at a potentially fantastic crossroad? Are we open to discovering the ways in which what we do and what we teach tutors to do may, in fact, subvert our most dearly held beliefs, principles, sense of ethos? These kinds of questions bump up against traditional tutor preparation in uncomfortable ways, just as Trickster's "'language of accidents' rubs the 'language of essences' the wrong way, creating a kind of mischief language that is always up to something, revealing accidents, coincidences, and contingencies" (Hyde 95). The result is a shape-shifting writing center practice, one that is not easily pinned down.

THAT'S THE ESSENCE OF IT: TRICKSTER IN A COMMUNITY OF PRACTICE

The language of writing center essences, we would argue, involves reification, a process "of giving form to our experience by producing objects that congeal this experience into 'thingness'" (Wenger 58). "We project our meanings into the world," Wenger writes, "and then we perceive them as existing in the world, as having a reality of their own" (58). Understanding the term *meaning*, as Wenger uses it, is central to an understanding of his project, and he places the concept in relation to an exploration of practice that leads us to conclude that practice is not simply what we do, which is how we often speak of it (particularly in relation to "theory"). It is, instead, "first and foremost a process by which we can experience the world and our engagement with it as meaningful" (51). From here, Wenger explains that the process involves an ongoing "negotiation of meaning" (52) taking place largely between the centrifugal pull of reification and the centripetal push of participation. Unchecked, reification promotes an "excessive concreteness" (Wenger 59) that potentially precludes a more improvisational, in-the-moment response to the diversity of experiences and everyday acts. And participation must be a conscious act, especially when we may not even be aware of all that keeps us in a cycle of reification absent participation.

Our ideas about one another may be structured and concretized in our unconscious minds, and yet we act upon these ideas as if they are true. In this sense we may order our lives—and our work—around ideas that we would eschew if we were aware of them. In his book, *Blink* Malcolm Gladwell describes the productive and destructive potential of the unconscious mind in the quickest decisions we make during the course of a day. With particular regard to identity, Gladwell notes that our received "immediate, automatic associations" may "tumble out before we've even had time to think," and, he suggests, "our unconscious attitudes may be utterly incompatible with our stated conscious values" (85). Trickster may, in a moment, flash before us some realization of the import and impact of an array of unconscious meanings embedded in our practices. But the deep-change significance of those moments is ours to discover and name. Trickster, Hyde says, is shameless (153). He will say aloud that which is forbidden. "If rules of silence help 'maintain the real'," Hyde writes, ". . . then one takes considerable risk breaking them." (157) Trickster does not name in order to create change; he names out of curiosity, cunning, mischief, or hunger. When we are able to pursue the broken silence rather than turn away from it in fear or shame, then we may begin both to participate more fully in the (re)negotiation of meaning (especially around identity) and to invest more fully in that (re)negotiation of the principles we espouse and the responsibility we believe we bear.

Warning: Trickster moments may raise identity matters, but not every disruption of the everyday is a sign that Trickster suddenly walked in the door; in fact, some of the moments of disruption which strike us might have to be seen for what they are–eruptions of racism, sexism, homophobia, able-ism, etc. Some serious disruptions–especially those revealing historical and structural inequities—may require a different mind. Trickster tickles and stimulates us as a conceptual frame for understanding the everyday. But like any conceptual frame, his use value in the everyday is not universal but particular, and contingent on circumstance and issue. Our experiences have taught us to be wary of those moments when a turn toward Trickster might have been, in fact, a turn away from engagement in deeper (and riskier) learning.

Hyde writes that "the intelligence that takes accidents seriously is a constant threat to essences, for, in the economy of categories, whenever the value of accident changes, so, too, does the value of essence" (100). Therefore, important cases exist in which the interplay of accident and essence can never be seen as balanced. For example, the revelation of oppression may be an accident, but oppression itself never is. In order to make sense of the accidental revelation, to take the accident seriously, one must understand deeply the thing that is revealed–the social, political, economic forces in human history and the collision of subject formation with those forces. To say that oppression in any of its forms is often unintentional is not to say that it is ever accidental. Oppression is a product of human thought and action and its impact is directly related to what humans think and do in time. Trickster may bring us pleasure and in that pleasure distract us from the seriousness which must attend the making of meaning or grace from grave matters. This may be part of the trick being played upon us. In our chapter on anti-racism work in the writing center, we take up the matter of oppression using race and racism as the lens through which we can understand the role that mindful learning plays in struggling against all forms of oppression.

Cultivating both a Trickster mind *and* a readiness for mindful learning is complex and not what many of us have been schooled for. The ossifying tendencies of reification and premature cognitive commitment are fairly predictable outcomes of traditional schooling (Illich) and a more generalized reliance on technical rationality as Donald Schön describes it. Technical rationality is "the idea that practical competence becomes professional when its instrumental problem-solving is grounded in systematic, preferably scientific knowledge" (8). Many have noted the appeal of technical rationality, both in the field of education and in the field of composition studies.[4] When writing centers become more normative in their curricula, they are responding to the privileged position that scientific certainty holds in the university system and in academic culture at large. As Schön tells us, the "relative status [of] professions is largely correlated with the extent to which they are able to present themselves as rigorous practitioners of a science-based professional knowledge and embody in their schools a version of the normative professional curriculum" (9). Although writing center tradition resists a reliance on a predictable, deterministic model for tutoring, we are still subject to pressure from our institutions to justify our methods, models, and procedures in ways that would encourage such reliance. However, we need to constantly struggle to demonstrate, both to our tutors and our institutions, that technical rationality can neither predict nor explain the "intelligence that begins by being tacit and spontaneous" (Schön 25).

Doubly challenging is that the work we do as we reflect on Trickster moments to make sense of them, and to teach and learn from them, may also highlight and threaten our institutions' over-reliance on technical rationality. As Schön notes, "When a member of a bureaucracy embarks on a course of reflective practice, allowing himself to experience confusion and uncertainty, subjecting his frames and theories to conscious criticism and change, he may increase his capacity to contribute to significant organizational learning, but he also becomes, by the same token, a danger to the stable system of rules and procedures within which he is expected to deliver his technical expertise" (328). It is not surprising that we can notice Trickster moments, but it is in making sense of those moments for ourselves and for others that we may meet our greatest resistance.

In writing centers, we see the tendency toward technical rationality, toward the exclusion of messy Trickster moments, most directly in the proliferation of tutor training textbooks, and we worry that an over-reliance on these texts limits tutors' meaningful participation in their own learning.[4] We are concerned that tutors and directors, facing multiple pressures, may rely too heavily (as all of us do on occasion) on "technical" approaches to staff education. Familiar memes—don't write on the paper, don't speak more than the student-writer, ask non-directive questions—get passed among cohorts of writing tutors as gospel before they even interact with writers in an everyday setting. When this sort of hand-off occurs, these mindsets may actually discourage tutors from admitting or even *noticing* that on-the-ground practices contradict implicit or explicit writing center "policy." Those of us who use these texts must do so cautiously, or, as Ellen Langer explains, these "premature cognitive commitments [create] mindsets that we accept unconditionally, without considering or being aware of alternative forms" (93). "Once a person processes information unconditionally," according to Langer, "these now-accepted facts do not come up for reconsideration" (93). Ingesting sound bytes, axioms, and policies is easy; it is learning to unlearn, learning to be flexible in the face of newness, and learning deep listening that is hard. At those moments, we come to see that staff education practices that welcome a Trickster state of mind are even more important than we thought.

Let us take a moment to clarify our point here: we are not suggesting that staff education manuals should play no role in writing center tutor education; we are not claiming that they can't be (or aren't) used creatively and responsibly. We are, however, arguing that we must consider the balance between reification (as produced by texts, procedural manuals, and policy statements) and participation in our writing centers. We do so by paying attention to the interaction between reification and participation, by taking advantage of our unique position in our institutions, a position that gives us the freedom to go into the liminal spaces Trickster inhabits. Schön, for example, suggests that we can—and must—learn "from a careful examination of artistry, that is, the competence by which practitioners actually handle indeterminate zones of practice" (13), and if "we focus on the kinds of reflection-in-action through which practitioners sometimes make new sense of uncertain, unique or conflicted situations of practice, then we will assume neither that existing professional knowledge fits every case nor that every problem has a right answer" (Schön 39). Schön seems to be arguing, as we are, for a Trickster mind. Trickster, Hyde tells us, "regularly bumps into things he did not expect. He therefore seems to have developed an intelligence about contingency, the wit to work with happenstance" (95–96).

It is, then, the *ready* of a "ready, set, go" tutor preparation that we are interested in disrupting. By calling into question the practices we feel certain of, we invite Trickster to help us reveal the value of meaningful discomfort and to teach a kind of mindfulness to human interaction. In an effort to uncover the "power of mindful learning," as described by Ellen Langer, we want to move away from an over-reliance on tutoring manuals and to avoid all that is "mock" in our orientation practice.

THERE'S THE RUB: THE LANGUAGE OF WRITING CENTER ACCIDENTS

We have lots of examples in writing center literature of the language of writing center accidents rubbing up against the language of writing center essences (to paraphrase Hyde). Here, for example, is William Ramsey's post to the *Writing Center Journal* blog: [6]

> [Indeed] I've never found a protocol, template, or fixed heuristic schema that survives more than a minute of writing center work. What little I can predict of a session might take this shape: (1) The client asks questions prompting the session's agenda; (2) There is some probing, some getting onto the other's wavelength, some settling into personas that will socially guide the interaction; and (3) Then—well, things start moving, trundling, stumbling, creaking, or zigzagging along in no way I could have foreseen. The sum total of what I know about writing center sessions is this: when the ball bounces—one goes for it. (March 28, 2005)

Using a different analogy, Stuart, a geography student, represents (in a drawing created during a writing center staff meeting) the average writing center conference as a river. Two streams meet at the beginning of the conference, and Stuart labels that intersection "different currents." Together student and tutor move to create a river where, through the "rapid flow," introductions, ideas and shared information intermingle in a mass of arrows moving forward. At the middle of the conference, and at the middle of this drawing, is the rocky flow, where riverbed dirt and debris are kicked up. Movement through those rapids can be fun and invigorating. On the other side of that rocky flow, Stuart depicts conferences "ambling" before going "out to sea."

In his chapter "Matter Out of Place," Hyde considers the indeterminacy of dirt (or debris, if you will), expanding a definition of dirt to include "not just what is out of place but what has no place at all when we are done making sense of our world" (176). Certainly, guidelines for responsible tutoring practice help to maintain a certain order, but we shouldn't go so far as to imagine that nothing is getting swept under the rug in the process. "[D]irt and order are mutually dependent," writes Hyde. As such, "[d]irt is one of the tools available to Trickster as he makes this world" (177). As we move through intellectual rapids, we must accept that dirt and debris will inevitably be churned up, and that is part of the challenge of this work. Increasing our tolerance for dirt is one way to guard against what Hyde terms "obsessive caretaking," an impulse that might have us peremptorily discarding things (or moments or people) we should otherwise take a hard look at. Hyde challenges us with these questions:

> How much control can we have before the good life we're guarding . . .
> ceases to be good in any conventional sense? Can we reduce contingency
> to zero, or must we always have some exposure to things we cannot con-
> trol? Is the life that has no risk a human life? (106)

These Trickster habits of mind have not come easily or naturally to all of us. The five of us have together lined the pockets of any number of publishers hawking their tutor-training wares. And we have had our own epiphanies, Trickster-like moments when we have been forced to look opportunity in the eye.

On occasion, our presentations of reified knowledge, textbook approaches to potential tutoring scenarios, have been met with unlikely acts of participation. For example, one attempt to teach out of *The Practical Tutor* elicited resistance from a number of participants in the room. A scribbled note passed from one tutor to another ("This is bullshit!"), crumpled up and pitched in the garbage near the door, confirmed truths we were beginning to suspect. On that day, what promised to be following the bouncing ball through the pages of a tutor-training manual felt like searching for that errant ball in a thicket of weeds. If, as Hyde points out, "the origins, liveliness, and durability of cultures require that there be space for figures whose function is to uncover and disrupt the very things that cultures are based on" (9), then Trickster was at our table that day, initiating our revision of writing center culture.

Once uttered, "bullshit" can not be retracted, so why not move forward? We can let it push us to find out what tutors recognize about training manuals, what tutors suspect about a director's claims to authority, and what directors begin to realize about received tutor-training methods and materials. Reading philosopher Harry G. Frankfurt's *On Bullshit*, we are reminded of this tutor's observation. One of the connotations of "bull" is "hot air," so, as Frankfurt writes:

> When we characterize talk as hot air, we mean that what comes out of the speaker's mouth is only that. It is mere vapor. His speech is empty, without content. His use of language, accordingly, does not contribute to the purpose it purports to serve. No more information is communicated than if the speaker had merely exhaled. (42–43)

Our conspiratorial tutors were right: using *The Practical Tutor* exercises that day was bullshit, hot air. Contrived, condescending, meaningless. Void of context, void of human interaction, void of the life experiences of both tutor and writer. In their vacuousness, our shortcomings were exposed. "Bullshitting," according to Frankfurt, "involves a kind of bluff" and that "[b]luffing . . . is typically devoted to conveying something false" (46). Rather than being completely false, however, bullshit is more akin to "fakery," since, as Frankfurt clarifies, "the essence of bullshit is not that it is false but that it is phony" (47). An over-reliance on canned tutor-training methods leads to a phony certification of our tutors, and thus, to more bullshit:

> Bullshit is unavoidable whenever circumstances require someone to talk without knowing what he is talking about. Thus the production of bullshit is stimulated whenever a person's obligations or opportunities to speak on some topic exceed knowledge of the facts that are relevant to that topic. This discrepancy is common in public life, where people are frequently impelled—whether by their own propensities or by the demands of others—to speak extensively about matters of which they are to some degree ignorant. (63)

Developing a Trickster habit of mind, recognizing moments of opportunity, involves facing hard truths about ourselves. It means fishing that crumpled note out of the garbage and taking it to heart. We could certainly have justified dismissing that tutor's frustrated proclamation. We could have placed the blame squarely on him—as resistant, disengaged, a trouble-maker. Those characterizations could be true. What could also be true, however, is this: that tutor could be right. Trickster requires us to imagine that *all* of those interpretations could be right, simultaneously. What do we do with that realization?

Our concern about an over-reliance on a training curriculum for tutors stems from the replacement of philosophy (embracing the "ordinary questions of the everyday") with expertise (a "competence transmuted into social authority"). The result of this trade? "[T]he more authority the Expert has, the less competence he has" (de Certeau 7). The false assumption that expertise (conferred by tutor training manuals, for example) leads to competence ("I know how to tutor every writer") interrupts the possibility of learning from these Trickster moments and effectively creates tutors who bluff and bluster. When de Certeau calls for "[t]he critical return of the ordinary" (13) or Spellmeyer urges us to return to "ordinary, sensuous life," they are both discouraging us from reveling in "all the varieties of rhetorical brilliance associated with powers that hierarchize and with nonsense that enjoys authority" (de Certeau 13).

In the writing center, beginning tutors often long for the safety of a text that can comfort them with a "toolbox" full of no-fail strategies and quick, easy answers. Like our *WCJ* blogger, however, the tutors soon discover that the task isn't that simple. Here, for example, is a journal entry from Jay, one of our tutors who clearly understands the connections among contingency, risk, and the "ordinary, sensuous life" about which Spellmeyer talks:

> Life is a hard thing to do. And by that I don't mean just getting through your days and relationships in one piece is hard, but actually doing things that make you feel alive, shaking things up, taking risks while thinking that maybe this will ruin everything but then again maybe this is exactly what is right and necessary. That's a hard thing to do. It's much easier to do what maintains a certain comfort level, getting by . . . . But that doesn't make anyone happy.
>
> That doesn't let anyone be happy.

In the same entry, Jay concludes, "In biology we learned that things naturally fall into disorder. That's the natural state of things. I'm in love. I told Nicole I feel healthy. Like everything's in its place. Which is something like everything being in chaos." In tutoring, the replication of a strategy-driven practice makes us dull, bored, depressed. Jay's right: it's much easier to maintain the comfort level by buying into the illusion that all contingency is contained within the pages of a manual, within the session reports, within the reporting lines; but without the risk that Hyde talks about, the bounce that Ramsey urges us to "go for," how can we practice our craft in a fully human(e) way?

SHAPE-SHIFTING, JOINT-DISTURBING, AND BRICOLAGE IN THE CENTER

At the 2005 Conference on College Composition and Communication, Erec Smith, the writing center director at Drew University, associated Trickster with the roles we play as teachers and tutors, roles that preclude measurement and careful containment. Stating that Trickster truly and simply "represents human interaction," Smith outlined several roles Trickster plays in our daily work: shape-shifter, messenger, bricoleur. Trickster personifies, then, a brand of practice that "makes claims not to a Truth or validity, but to viability and efficacy in relation to a particular audience and intention within a particular situation" (Ellsworth qtd. in Kopelson 115). In this way, Trickster privileges participation over reification. When we allow Trickster to work in these ways in our writing centers, we are better able to balance these two tendencies in a manner that fosters true engagement in a learning community.

We can all recognize the characters on our stage: the shape-shifter disguises of our tutors, the "cultural informant" role of messenger for new English speakers, the bricoleur who is able to build something out of seemingly nothing. In the final section of this chapter, we offer some thoughts on these roles as we have discussed their operations in our writing centers. We don't mean this discussion to be an extensive or exhaustive consideration of all of the ways Trickster shifts shapes or disturbs joints in a writing center. Rather, we hope readers will recognize moments like these in their own centers and identify the gaps, the things not yet said, in the following examples.

Shape-shifters

According to Hyde, Trickster is a "pore-seeker" and "keeps a sharp eye out for naturally occurring opportunities and creates them ad hoc when they do not occur by themselves" (47). If this is true, then we block opportunities for ourselves, for our tutors, and for writers each time we invoke our familiar "do's and don'ts." Sure, "[t]rickster can get snared in his own devices" (Hyde 19), but often this ensnarement is just one step in the "incremental creation of intelligence" (Hyde 10). Attending to Trickster in our centers helps tutors to think creatively about how to free themselves from an unwitting snare. While it is easy for any director to critique the rules and boundaries set in a writing center we don't direct, we do wonder about unyielding rules given to tutors. Rules like "never say what you think of the professor's comments" or "never change a word that the student has written to one of your own." We prefer instead to hear a barely articulated concern or criticism, seize it, and work with the tutors to claim it. For example, an admission by one of the tutors that she feared she had "gone too far" (i.e. done too much work for the student) in a session led us to set a goal for all the tutors. Instead of nodding knowingly at this tutor's admission, affirming that yes, indeed, there was such a thing as going too far and she had in fact done that, we issued this challenge: Before the next staff meeting, have a moment with a student where you consciously decide to go too far. Pay attention to that moment, to what led up to it, to what followed it, to any perceived concerns or consequences. The following staff meeting was devoted to a discussion and examination of those moments.

When directors step in as Tricksters, we model for tutors ways that a Trickster mindset can be brought to bear on their interactions with each other and with writers in the writing center. As they learn to expose assumptions about themselves and their own work, they begin to shape-shift to rhetorical Other with writers, interrupting a session to make explicit a student's effort to obfuscate or deny the value of contrasting evidence, the playful what-ifs. In these ways, Trickster nudges tutors and students from their comfort zones to acknowledge new voices and countervailing forces within texts, arguments, and research findings.

Joint-disturbers

Like the shape-shifting Trickster, the joint-disturbing Trickster toys with some of our most sacred binaries: certainty and uncertainty; knowledge and ignorance; change and stability; boundaries and fluidity. In particular, Tricksters like the "*flexible* or *moveable* joint" (Hyde 246). Like Trickster, writing centers have worked to "reshape [by] disjointing, rejointing the world around them" (Hyde 257).

Perhaps Trickster can instigate a deeper understanding of both our complicity with institutional practices and our efforts to step around these practices. By shifting familiar patterns and re-articulating order, we make an attractive site for Trickster to enact "cultural hybridity" and to more easily "cross linguistic borders"; Trickster as joint-disturber is "the hunger-artist who inhabits the cracks between languages" (Hyde 260). Writing center staff members recognize that, within their daily work, moments that are both "connecting/not connecting" present themselves—whether found in the local arrangement of tutor and student writer, or in more global speculation as to where and how writing centers are connected to their institutions.

Two examples from our own writing centers, both involving seemingly benign decisions to adorn the spaces with text-based images, demonstrate the regulatory impulse to eliminate the dirt of contingency and reveal the Trickster's tendency to be "a character of ambivalence and duplicity . . . echoing the duality of human existence" (Spinks 81). The first incident involves the magnetic poetry that has become a staple design element in the homes and offices of the literary-minded across the country and that has also found its way into our writing centers. As a tutor broke apart all the pieces of the new set and began to put them up on the filing cabinet, we glanced over, only to realize that some of the fun magnetic poetry words were offensive. Suddenly, buying that second box of magnetic poetry titled "Slang" seemed like a very, very bad idea. We took down some of the more offensive words, hesitated, left some of the questionable ones, and shook our heads.

The next day, we overheard the tutors laughing loudly in the writing center. Of course, they were all drawn to the magnetic words. But what are we as writing center directors if we let a fear of words keep us from our work? Aren't writing centers spaces where censorship and profanity should be discussed openly? Places where one person's profanity can be another person's poetry? Where's the line? Well, we don't know if we don't talk about it, and if we don't talk about it, we know that Trickster will appear, invited or not. A student will use a word that a tutor or a professor finds unacceptable. The ball starts to bounce. Who responds and how?

And so it was that only one tutor was brave enough to whisper in the director's ear the meaning of the word everyone was laughing about. As words on the filing cabinet were pointed at and explained, it became clear that the meaning was not the same for everyone standing about. Beyond that, nouns from the less dangerous generic magnetic poetry could take on unintended meanings when set alongside and between seemingly innocuous prepositions and verbs. Words and phrases that appeared to be fixed, fastened quite firmly to the side of that cabinet, loosened up as we worked them. As Hyde observes, "[W]hat Tricksters quite regularly do is create lively talk where there has been silence, or where speech has been prohibited" (76).

The five of us thought through this mag-po incident together in relation to a similar exchange that had occurred a few years earlier. This one involved a senior faculty member who had invaded the writing center with a group of others in tow. "This is a disgrace," she proclaimed, regarding a piece of donated student artwork on the wall. "Isn't this a disgrace?" she asked the others, as though the appropriate response were still negotiable. Without drawing any closer to where we were seated in the office, she nonetheless hailed us, through tone and register, demanding, "Where did you get this? It needs to be taken down. It's a disgrace. I mean, I think it's really a disgrace." The artwork in question is a two-piece installation: one a shadowbox with round objects and an image of a boy and girl in an elementary school classroom; the other a five-foot high computer print-out, in binary code, with words tracing the human life span from birth to death. It's an intriguing study of text and image, containing one or possibly two unfortunate words: *fuck* (which, truth be told, many humans do—and quite enjoy—in the course of their lives) and *masturbate* (again, common enough in practice).

Later that same afternoon, another group was marched down to the writing center to examine this same piece; this second group was led by us and consisted of the students enrolled in that semester's writing center staff education class. Together, we considered both the power of literacy and the regulatory role played all too willingly by people who should know better. It is such regulation that we think is the true disgrace. Isn't that a disgrace? We think it's a disgrace. Again we turn to Hyde, who writes, "[U]sually language goes dead because cultural practice has hedged it in, and some shameless double-dealer is needed to get outside the rules and set tongues wagging again" (76).

Bumper sticker: *Linguistic Eruptions Happen.*

Trickster as Bricoleur

In what is perhaps an appropriate move for five would-be *bricoleuses*, we turned to Google Glossary, which led us to this explanation of the term:

> A French word with no exact English equivalent used as a term by Seymour Papert to describe the style of approach exemplified by a tinkerer or a jack

of all trades. Bricoleurs are comfortable in unfamiliar realms of learning and experience because they learn best by using indirect connections to known information, even if the details of the skills are not exactly related. They try things out until they figure out how to do something. (http://www.bricoleur.org)

In our conversations, we have each introduced the others to our longstanding and our short-term interests, and we have more than once surprised the group with unorthodox connections to our "ordinary sensuous" lives: practicing with clicker training, playing speed golf, or housebreaking a new puppy; renewing an old interest in drumming, hockey, or Texas Hold-Em; experiencing the birth of a new grandbaby, the death of an old friend. This tendency toward *bricolage* is perhaps what we five share as much as, if not more than, anything else. The connections to the work we do with our tutors, with writers, within our institutions are not always easy or seamless, but they are there, and we push each other to bring these connections to light. Many of them are here in the remaining chapters; more have been left around tables in Providence, Lawrence, Minneapolis, Louisville, and Chicago. They have all informed the work.

We have begun to establish in this chapter a central principle of this book: consonance and constancy. Tutors will work with writers in ways they themselves have been taught; directors then must make certain to work with tutors in ways tutors should work with writers. As directors, we too must seek out communities that challenge us to work in ways that are risky, fluid, hybrid. Otherwise, we will not be able to avoid the imposition of a more hierarchical, top-down model, even if only indirectly. Wenger establishes, as we noted in the introduction, that our communities of practice overlap, reinforcing, touching, and troubling each other. The same types of mindfulness we advocate for tutors in our centers, then, we must also develop for ourselves: directors, leaders, administrators, teachers.

Historically, the western intellectual tradition teaches us to gravitate toward certainty and to strive for Truth instead of valuing those moments when the foundations of our truths are rocked—those moments when Trickster plays with our sense and perception. The transformative potential of the Trickster moment is not purely in Trickster's actions or intentions, however. Rather, the possibility of learning and of being transformed by such moments lies in what sense we make of that flash of vision the Trickster moment gives us of ourselves, our convictions about who we are, what the world is and how and why it is just that way. We are well-schooled in ways to operate; it seems unless we can predict the outcomes of our choices, we won't make those choices, or we actually believe we can predict the outcomes of our choices when the variable is other human beings—the most unstable variable and the one from which we can and should attempt to learn the most. There almost certainly will be *jouissance* as we cultivate Trickster minds in the writing center, but there is also a certain *gravitas* that attends wandering the borders of the profane with Trickster. We may laugh wildly at Trickster's revelation of the mundane in practices we once held dear, but in those moments feel called again to redefine what might be transformative to our labor—our thinking and our talk—to our writing centers and our institutions. Trickster asks us to reflect on and perform in situations not accounted for in any training manual, employing a strength and intelligence capable of meeting the unexpected. We throw our Coyote eyes up into a tree and regard the world as it looks back at us.

3

BEAT (NOT) THE (POOR) CLOCK

Time is what a clock measures.
What a clock measures is more interesting than we thought.

Raphael Bousso

Think about how time works in your writing center. When does your staff—when do *you*—have too little time? Too much? If those questions are too abstract, try these: When do you think of time being wasted in the writing center? Why? How often do you check to see how many appointment slots are full and how many are empty? Do you allow students to schedule appointments any time they like, or do you, as one writing center we know, have a public policy that states: "If your paper is due in two hours or less, you cannot meet with a consultant. You will not have enough time to revise after your consultation." Do you even believe a writing center should decide how much time is the appropriate amount of time for revision? Is it more than two hours? More than two days? Why? Coyote sits in the doorway, waiting for your answers.

As you think about time with us throughout this chapter, we hope you will consider what types of time are valued in the everyday of the writing center where you spend *your* time. We've included this chapter because we know that it would be easy to say there's no time for what we suggest in this book. But here, at the very beginning of our discussion of this topic, we want to assert that our use of time and our conception of time can change and can be changed for the better.

One way to look at time is through the lens of work day productivity. When he describes the production reports filed by claims processors, Etienne Wenger notes that "limiting the report to numbers of claims processed is a way to enforce a specific, exportable interpretation on a day of work" (132). But, as Wenger points out,

> the number of claims processed that day leaves out much of what happened . . . A whole day of work, negotiation of meaning, boredom, inventiveness, rebellion, conversation, and community building has been reified into a number, which—even in terms of what has been done specifically for the company—is a very restricted representation of that day. (Wenger 132)

At the very heart of what we five have come to understand as we've talked about time is our belief that writing centers should be most focused on time that is relational. What would happen, for example, if we could stop worrying about making arguments about efficiency based on how many conference slots are filled? What would happen if we could imagine tutors' out–of-conference-time as some of the most important teaching time available to us and to them? What if we discovered that short conferences, or conferences held right before a due date (and we mean right before, as in the "I have an hour before class, could you look at this and I'll make changes before I hand it in" variety) could be as satisfying and productive for tutor and writer as long-term relationships? And what if writing centers were where tutors and directors could be "involved in becoming certain persons" together, rather than needing to be certain people from the start of our work with one another (Wenger 155)? Well, we might, we want to suggest, be able to teach those around us how to think about time in very different ways, to take long future-oriented views of our work, and to value exploration over efficiency.

00:00

We live by schedules and clocks. A syllabus is developed to fit the thirteen or fourteen (or, on the quarter system, seven or eight) weeks of the term. Learning, someone has decided, can fit into that pre-determined amount of time. Despite all the talk about assessment, no one seems to be assessing this fundamental assumption, though we know there is a distinct rhythm to the semester that we feel and our students feel.[1] We turn constantly to our watches or our cell phones and check the hour and the minute, or, in our offices, we glance to the corners of our computer screens, even when we're writing. This sort of timekeeping is the physical manifestation of a central tension we live with in writing centers—the tension between fungible time and epochal time. Fungible time is measured by "units . . . equivalent to and interchangeable with any of the other units. These units may take on the values of any clock or calendar interval (second, minute, hour, day, week, month, year, decade, century, etc.)" (Bluedorn 30). Epochal time, on the other hand, is measured by events—the "time is in the events; the events do not occur in time" (31). For example, following fungible time, when we are together as a group to work on this book, we often say "Let's quit working and go to sleep at midnight. That's a reasonable bedtime." In epochal time we write and talk and think until we can no more, and we say, "Let's go to sleep. We can't think clearly, and we can't make this paragraph work, so it must be time to go to sleep." In epochal time "the event defines the time," and time is "linked to the individual's internal rhythms" (e.g., fatigue) or "external social rhythms" (e.g., whether one of us can keep the others awake) (Bluedorn 31).

Alan Lightman makes a similar division in *Einstein's Dreams*, calling one time "mechanical time" and the other "body time" (23). Of those who follow the first, mechanical time, "those who think their bodies don't exist," he says, "When they begin to lose themselves in a concert, they look at the clock above the stage to see when it will be time to go home" (25). Shackled to mechanical time, they think the "body is a thing to be ordered, not obeyed" (26). Those who live in body time "listen to their heartbeats," "feel the rhythms of their moods and desires," and "eat when they are hungry" (24). "They know," Lightman writes,

> that time struggles forward with a weight on its back when they are rushing an injured child to the hospital or bearing the gaze of a neighbor wronged. And they know too that time darts across the field of vision when they are eating well with friends or receiving praise or lying in the arms of a secret lover. (25)

Why stop and think about these two types of time—mechanical time and body time—in the context of the writing center? Well, because we all live and work in a world that works against relational time. In the face of short writing center appointments (constantly threatened to become ever shorter because of budget cuts) and rushed students with busy schedules, we risk giving in to the pressure of fungible time. When we do, we may, without even noticing it or stopping to think about it, make rules and become more entrenched in timekeeping than we need to be. Timekeeping need not, in fact, be synonymous with clockwatching. We might remember that "keep" also means "to care for." We aim in this chapter to explore time in our writing centers as a way to demonstrate such caring.

If we are constrained by the clock time and disconnected from writers' time, our practices may end up contradicting our mission. How can we say we will work with writers at any stage in the writing process but then refuse to if the paper is due in "less" than "two hours"? Even though psychologist Robert Levine tells us, "A focus on people is often at odds with a tempo dictated by schedules and the time on the clock" (19), clocks are everywhere in writing centers, and we are more bound by them and to them than we might like to admit. It is difficult to work productively if we allow the hands of the clock to limit what we will and won't accept as the point of writers' needs. Time begins to function as an excuse, preventing us from having harder conversations about our responsibilities to each other (and about our priorities), interfering with our ability to exercise our own judgment, saving us from ourselves (by keeping us from doing too much work for students, for example).

Early writing process theorists frequently advocated brief, focused conferences with writers. We seem to have forgotten about Donald Murray's three- or four-minute conference rubric, or Roger Garrison's work that "recommends brief conferences (three to five minutes) focusing on a single problem that the student and tutor have identified as important" (277).[2] Although this strategic approach was born of time management concerns, we shouldn't ignore its corresponding pedagogical rationale: "Quality of time spent is more important than quantity of time. Students profit most from intensity" (Garrison 69). Much writing center literature stresses the easing in and rapport-building element of conferences, of swaddling the conference in a kind of comfort zone, keeping student anxiety at bay. As Grimm, Welch, McKinney and others have cautioned, however, we may be wrong in assuming a shared understanding of comfort; and our privileging of a leisurely conference unfolding between two equally invested participants may be one manifestation of that mistaken assumption. In fact, because time is experienced differently by different cultures, one person's timekeeping may be uncomfortable and unfamiliar to a person from another culture.[3]

Let's look instead at the possible values of a strategic intensity in a compressed time frame. What does it mean to ask tutors to define something doable when there is less time to ease into the conference, to prioritize student *and* text while setting an agenda quickly, to help students understand that a brief conference may need to focus on one aspect of the writing? Amazingly, Garrison was not speaking of writing centers when he said "the *most* effective teaching method is one-to-one tutorial . . . this kind of teaching is creative intervention . . . at times and in ways that can be most immediately useful" (69).

We have been captivated recently by the idea of speed in conferences. Our society is similarly enamored of speed. One need only look at the popularity of speed chess, speed golf, and speed dating in order to see interesting parallels emerge. For example, to foster what Malcolm Gladwell calls "thin slicing" (with this term offering an unintended joke for golfers), speed golf eradicates a common syndrome: analysis paralysis. Over-thinking the shot is not possible when the demands are intensified, and "in speed golf, due to the accelerated pace of play, players

MUST stay in the present. Players become more aware of their strengths and weaknesses during a round of speed golf, quickly learning to capitalize on their strengths." With a narrower and more intentional club selection and a focus not on completing the course in less time, but in making the most of the time spent, Christopher Smith[4] claims:

> You don't have a lot of time to think, so you must play the game instinctively, by feel. Most of what hurts amateur golfers is they play with mechanical thoughts, no rhythm and no feeling. This game forces you to play with pictures and images, the way the best golfers in the world do.

Our tutors, products as they are of our culture of speed, without doubt can teach us something about the tension between speed and slowness, if we are willing to give them space and attention. At the end of the fall semester, for example, Bryan, one of our tutors, told everyone in the staff meeting that he wanted to talk about a conference he had held that week. "It might have been one of the best I've had this semester," he said. The story had a back-story, a narrative of how tired Bryan had been that day from his own graduate work and how much coffee he'd drunk before arriving at the writing center for his shift—too much coffee, he said. For the past few weeks the staff had been warning the new consultants of student requests that might arise in conferences—or at the gym, or on the pathways between academic buildings—at the end of the semester. Those warnings foretold of students who would be needy this time of the semester, behind on their deadlines. They forget to make appointments; they will stop you anywhere and ask you for your help. You may certainly say no outside the writing center. Students will come to the writing center right before their writing is due. Don't feel pressured. Do whatever you feel is right in conference with the time you know you have. These conversations were about teaching tutors to think about time and teaching decisions in relation to one another; these conversations were about developing what Wenger calls "shared repertoire," a "community's set of shared resources" that "reflects a history of mutual engagement" and "remains inherently ambiguous" (82–83).

Wenger explains further: "The repertoire of a community of practice includes routines, words, tools, ways of doing things, stories, gestures, symbols, genres, actions or concepts that the community has produced or adopted in the course of its existence, and which have become a part of its practice" (83). A community's repertoire "is the resource for the negotiation of meaning," and "mutual engagement" does not rely solely on "literally shared meaning" (83). So, as a community of practice reflects on its shared repertoire, "mismatched interpretations or misunderstandings need to be addressed and resolved directly only when they interfere with mutual engagement. Even then, they are not merely problems to resolve, but occasions for the production of new meanings" (83). It is "useless," Wenger reminds us, "to try to excise all ambiguity" (remember our Tricksters), so we must "situate ambiguity in the context of a history of mutual engagement that is rich enough to yield an opportunity for negotiation" (84).

"Really, it might have been one of the best conferences I've had this semester," Bryan said again to the tutors he had been talking with, and thinking with, for months. When the student came in with the my-paper-is-due-in-an-hour routine, Bryan, all hepped up on coffee, was up for the challenge. They were able to focus intensely, he reported, and work together. He felt as if his own end-of-the-semester pressure, his own over-caffeination, had helped him work within and with the student's (un)realistic time schedule. They prioritized together. He let her decide which sections of her text they should pay attention to; and, with his short attention span, he let the other sections go without much thought. He and the student agreed to stop with twenty minutes of the conference to spare so she could turn to one of the writing center's computers and make a few changes. "It was great," he told everyone. We laughed and laughed. Though it might not have been apparent in our previous chapter, Trickster moments such as this one are often filled with humor. It is in these eruptions that the cracks we so often straddle—last-minute or no last-minute conferences, for example—become evident. The warnings handed out over the past few weeks had not predicted that a last-minute, down-to-the-wire conference could be satisfying, but the warnings had also not been rules excluding that possibility.

In *Time for Life*, John Robinson and Geofrey Godbey write that instead of "timesaving skills, we need to cultivate *time-savoring* skills" (316). "To be happier and wiser," they claim, "it is easier to increase appreciation levels more than efficiency levels. Only by appreciating *more* can we hope to have a sustainable society" (316). While efficiency, "at least as envisioned by American society, always starts with *wanting* more, appreciating may start both with *valuing* more about what is already here and with wanting less" (316, emphasis original). We may want writers to visit the writing center when they have more time, but that will not always happen. In Bryan's case, instead of sending the student away with her needs unmet (which he could have done), he engaged her productively in a manner that signaled an appreciation and a valuing of the time they could spend together. This lesson, we believe, is worth discussing with our staffs: How do we savor whatever time we have? Those of us who direct writing centers should be asking these same questions of ourselves: What is possible if we appreciate and value whatever time we have–for reading, for research, for our own professional and intellectual growth?

00:15

By the clock, there may not be enough time for everything we want to do. Conferences are too short to finish all the work we'd like to complete with student writers. We have too little time in our staff education courses to feel certain the students are ready, really *ready* (whatever that means), to begin tutoring on their own. Some of our tutors work fewer hours or not as many semesters as we'd wish. They go away on study abroad, or they selfishly graduate, leaving us with newer, less experienced tutors, who actually do need more time to feel knowledgeable and comfortable in the writing center. We teach and have campus responsibilities, and we feel that we don't have enough time for our research, or even to read. Because many of us are women, and/or family caregivers, we feel caught in what Arlie Hochschild so aptly named "the time bind." We carry student texts home and read them after children go to sleep. We read and respond to emails from our staff at all hours of the day and night. We imagine a day when we have enough time for everything we want to do, as if that day could actually arrive.

We divide ourselves into what Hochschild calls "real" and "potential" selves, "aware of the fact that we have more things to do than time to do them" (235). "A potential self," according to Hochschild, "is a set, not of imagined present alternatives—activities one 'might have done' or ways 'one might have been'—but of imagined future possibilities" (235). The haves and the have-nots, "fantasy creations of time-poor" writing center directors who long to be "time-millionaires" (235), always willing, like the employees of Hochschild's Amerco, "to forge exciting plans" with "no time to carry out any of them" (236). Writing center directors seem to divide themselves into two categories: those who say they have *no time to be in* the writing center (other responsibilities/research, etc.) and those who say they have *no time to be out of* the writing center (must tutor, must be present at all times to supervise/be seen): If I'm not in the writing center, I don't spend enough time there to know what's going on. If I *am* in the writing center, I don't have enough time to do my work.

The five of us try never to find ourselves in one or the other category, but that does not mean it is easy or comfortable for us to make choices about where and how to spend our time.

00:30

"If we do not understand time, we become its victims," James Gleick writes in *Faster*. Most of us take time, and timekeeping, for granted. It would be easy to read this chapter as championing speed (at times) or seeking slowness (at others), but what we're suggesting is that careful attention to the everyday may require both speed and slowness, the ability to expand and contract time in conferences and in our institutional dealings.

We wonder whether we can *perform* time. What if we took up Geoffrey Sirc's idea of "composition as a Happening"? Based on Allan Kaprow's experimental theatre of the mid-20th century, "Happenings" exemplify "*event* time, when the activity itself has a set sequence and all the steps of the sequence must be completed no matter how long (or short) the elapsed time clock" (Schechner 8). Could a tutoring session following that set sequence be viewed more as an event, like a baseball game or a rain dance? Things take as long as they take. As performance theorist Schechner reminds us, "In performance activities, *time is adapted to the event*, and is therefore susceptible to numerous variations and creative distortions" (8).

Frequent discussions, on the WCenter listserv and elsewhere, are focused on time in the writing center and invariably revolve around questions about the most appropriate session length. Directors ask other directors how they keep their tutors from running over time in conferences, and we reassure one another that conferences in which we focus on just one skill are preferable. In our staff meetings, we raise the issue of time management over and over again. If, however, we approach time as a performative concept, if we assume a Happening perspective, we shift the terms of the conversation a bit, changing it from an assessment of what we do (or don't) have enough time for to an exploration of what we value and prioritize in each conference and why. If we recognize and harness the types of abilities developed through the experience of tutoring, we see opportunities to nurture a particular kind of intelligence. This intelligence stems from the kind of timely responsiveness required in an environment unlike any other at our institutions—an environment designed expressly to be responsive at the point of need. Yet we see our writing center tutors struggle with dueling demands: meeting the job guidelines ("We only have thirty minutes together.") while running with their intuition or emotional intelligence about how long the session may need to be in order for the student writer to truly "get it" ("I feel bad that we had to stop. We were on a roll."). Robert J. Sternberg, author of *Thinking Styles*, claims that "the essence of intelligence would seem to be in knowing when to think and act quickly, and knowing when to think and act slowly" (qtd. in Gleick 114).

Expanding and contracting time to optimize learning about writing is something we believe our tutors actually do quite well; this almost automatic action and adjustment relies on a kind of "thin-slicing," a skill defined by Malcolm Gladwell as "the ability of our unconscious to find patterns in situations and behavior based on very narrow slices of experience" (23). As that tutor's six or ten hours a week of authentic experiences build toward expertise, "rapid cognition" can kick in as needed. Watch your tutors "gather the necessary information for a sophisticated judgment [that] is automated, accelerated [and] unconscious" (23). Observe them "sifting through the situation . . . throwing out all that is irrelevant while zeroing in on what really matters" (34). Thin-slicing is perhaps best employed under circumstances that seem "fleeting"—a familiar description of the instant and temporary relationships we create every day in our writing centers. Gladwell claims, "[O]ur unconscious is really good at this, to the point where thin-slicing often delivers a better answer than more deliberate and exhaustive ways of thinking" (34). Remember Bryan in his hyper-caffeinated state?

It's not only our tutors who thin-slice. We do it too, and we're coming clean about it. Among the five of us, one guilty admission turned to surprise when we learned, in our early conversations about time in the writing center, that not a single one of us formally observes tutors in session. We catch a 20–second exchange on our way to the bookshelf, a 60–second conversation as we heat our lunch or juggle our bags and unlock the office door, a tense 3–minute negotiation as we unjam the printer or run files off of the database. Despite this, when we offer our assessment of an overheard session, the low tones of which drift into our office spaces periodically, our tutors grin and respond, "You really do know everything that goes on in here, don't you?" We've had tutors say, "I knew you would say something about that conference," when they've realized the director's office door had been open throughout sessions. What we value the most, perhaps, is the type of peer response that grows from this modeling. We like nothing more than to hear one tutor say, for example, "I already talked with Abigail about that conference. She overheard a few minutes of it."

00:45

Let us clarify here. We are not advocating that we overtly teach tutors to run a speedy or a slow conference. Instead, we observe in our work that tutors live time differently, depending to some extent on their experience and expertise. And we have come to believe that theorizing time with tutors can help them and us to keep options open, can allow them and us to summon different performances.

For example, we've observed the following scene repeatedly in staff education courses or meetings. The new tutors bring drafts to the group and are instructed to respond to each other's work. After twenty minutes, they look up, task complete, ready to move on to the next activity. "That took you twenty minutes," we report. "In the writing center, you would have an hour to do that work." Shock and dismay wash over faces across the room. They can't imagine, quite literally, how to talk about one paper for an hour. These same tutors, the next semester, will consistently need 70, 75, 90 minutes to do their work, despite the writing center's (admittedly arbitrary) one-hour appointment blocks. Soon enough, the tutors settle in, and the best among them, come graduation, can expand and contract a session with the skill and ease of an accordion-player in a zydeco band—15 minutes here, 40 minutes there.

In our own writing centers, we began our exploration of time first by noticing—noticing the central role of clocks in tutors' artistic depictions of their writing center experiences; noticing the unfolding of the writing center's history through tutor journals; reading broadly and deeply about time; and recognizing opportunities to use those theories in our work with tutors. From there, we have all, to varying degrees, both formally and informally, made the investigation of time in the writing center an explicit concern of our staff education opportunities. We draw on our own experiences with time to bring our tutors into conversation.

Imagine a speed chess game. The clock set tight, even five minutes per player, invites a kind of slam-dunk chess, a frenzy of hands banging the clock top and lifting pieces out of the way simultaneously, a hungry way of looking at the board, taking it all in more rapidly, loud music playing in the room, both players standing up. No more hands holding heavy heads up for an hour; instead, time is spent challenging the players at a very different game.

Now imagine a chess clock on a writing center table set at, say, fifteen minutes on both clocks. Following each conversational move, the speaker presses the stopper down, which then begins the partner's clock. Back and forth words, questions, explanations. The two look at the time left on each side when they have had their say: Whose red flag fell first, signaling that time has run out? Who forgot to hit the clock? Eventually time falls away as both players agree to give it up, ignore it, let the battery die.

Or maybe a three-minute egg timer sits on the main tutoring table. Struck by how long it took for all of the sand to filter to the bottom of the hourglass, we wondered whether tutors would feel the same way. At points in the semester when new tutors were racing through their sessions, the egg timer seemed as if it might be a helpful reminder of how slowly three minutes can actually drain. During the next staff meeting, tutors were instructed to use the egg timer at any point in any session in any way they deemed appropriate. The egg timer did indeed have the effect of helping the tutors to slow down sessions that seemed to be spiraling out of control. They used the timer in a variety of ways: to break for parallel writing time, to set the paper aside and simply talk (during times when the tutor felt she was too focused on the text), to attend to a student's concerns about grammatical correctness while also addressing broader textual features, and to encourage a discussion of a student's writing history and experiences (for tutors who have a tendency to dive right into a session with no preliminary conversation).

With our concern for speed, efficiency, and squeezing every second 'til it squeals, we shortchange ourselves most, perhaps, in the missed opportunities for real reflection. A part of making work, and the time we have for it, expandable is finding time for reflection within the time we already don't have. One way to do this is to make a consideration of time—and opportunities for reflection about time in the writing center—an explicit part of our staff education throughout the year, using not simply an isolated activity like the egg timer one above but a systematic plan that encourages tutors to make time a consistent part of their exploration of writing center work.

When time is designated as the official theme for an annual staff retreat, for instance, one student dresses up as rapper Flavor Flav, clock necklace and all. Time becomes the focus of staff discussion and theorizing, popping up over and over again at surprising moments—in a research project that included a survey of students, in tutors' written responses to a variety of prompts, in their choice of a superpower ability to manipulate time for their designated writing center superheroes. Here, for example, is Moira Ozias (a writing center assistant director) writing a summary of the findings from a survey of students on the benefits of writing center sessions and what might be done differently:

These responses indicate that students experience time as a very real dimension that affects their writing and their success as writers. Many students, however, may not be making connections between their learning and writing, and the ways they experience (and use?) time. The discrepancy between responses to the questions highlights an interesting tension between what students experience and need as writers and what they're learning to identify as their growing points. The discrepancy should also prompt consultants to think about how they use, experience, and become more aware of time in sessions and how they talk about this with other writers.

Noel, a graduate writing consultant, writes about what continues to challenge her:

> It is an ongoing struggle to believe in thirty minutes as a vast expanse of time—because my sense is that if I felt calmer about what could be accomplished in that time, I'd be more comfortable with being quiet as students puzzle out changes on their own before I jump in with suggestions.

With this deliberate attention to time throughout the year, naturally we started to notice our expressions and attitudes toward time. For example, do we really mean to "kill time" when not working with a student writer? A comprehensive approach to asking such questions about time might take several forms, from a three-minute freewrite to a day-long retreat with Time as its theme. One activity that grew out of such a retreat asked tutors to list the things they do to "kill time." Here's Nate, adding his two tongue-in-cheek cents to the question, "How do tutors best 'kill time' in the writing center?" by listing the benefits of his down time:

- getting to know your colleagues
- feeling more comfortable in the work environment
- sharing ideas on consulting, NASCAR, education, work itself, fast food, or
- whatever else is on the teeming minds of consultants
- establishing a network between like-minded individuals
- being able to ask questions of the others
- learning more about what you do

And a sample of downtime activities compiled during his downtime:

⌛ reading

⌛ writing

⌛ daydreaming

⌛ deep reflection

⌛ complaining

⌛ drinking coffee

⌛ organizing my binder

⌛ researching morbid professions or rare neurological conditions

⌛ tying my shoes

⌛ homework

⌛ and in this case, writing my practicum presentation.

STOP: PAUSE

Writing center work is "caring" work, and the work of compassion and the hands of a clock rarely neatly square. As Karen Davies, a feminist geographer, reminds us, "an emphasis upon . . . [a] resource-based notion of time . . . fails to fully account for a relational construction of time," a construction of time "shaped by . . . caring" (133). Relationally, according to Davies, we determine how to "best act in a certain situation . . . [by our] own judgment and understanding of the needs of the other—rather than upon a bureaucratic and economic reality" (139). Tutors' conferences, for example, run over-time so often because tutors are more worried about fulfilling the needs of the writer than they are about the bureaucratic schedule of the writing center. By extension, tutors may resist taking time during conferences for reflection because they worry, in doing so, that they are wasting precious time or selfishly spending time on themselves.

"There's never a spare moment," Davies subtitles a section of her essay, and the conflict as she sees it is that "reflexivity in the late modern age requires time—or a 'pause'" (133). It is unlikely, as Davies shows by considering day care centers and nursing units, that caregivers will choose a pause for reflection over other-oriented work when time is limited. In all care-giver professions, "activities cannot be neatly scheduled" and "time for reflection and time for oneself . . . by necessity get put aside" (143). "Spatially," she adds, "it is difficult to leave those who cannot care for themselves and concentrate on one's thought" (143). No wonder tutors, who see writers as needing them, are hesitant to claim any portion of conferences for their own needs, for their own reflection. If tutors see writers' needs as the most important needs in a conference, why would they ignore those needs to find time for pauses for themselves?

Yet it is taking a pause, creating space for reflection inside and outside of conferences, that allows tutors to feel they are in control of time and their own decisions rather than feeling as if their decisions are controlled by time. Through experience, tutors learn how to work these pauses into conferences informally, excusing themselves to think about the conference even while in the midst of it. We have witnessed experienced consultants leaving a conference to get tea for themselves and writers. During the busiest times, tutors might sneak bathroom breaks, occasions that turn out, as often as not, to really be about changing the pace, pacing the hall, or dipping outside for a breath of air. Davies found day care workers happy to wash dirty dishes, because it gave them time away from the children to think about their work. But we believe, and Davies believes, these pauses are more effective if we learn to name these pauses explicitly for reflection and take them in the midst of our responsibilities.

Davies calls for a commitment to others that is "built upon reciprocity, rather than dependency" (146). She notes when a caregiver is denied reflexivity essential to development, relationships of dependency may also deny the possibility of more equal caregiving and caretaking. More equal relationships in turn would create space for reflexivity, even for the caregiver. If Davies is right, as we think she is, the more a tutor is willing to claim a pause, the more balanced and generative a tutor-writer relationship may become. By encouraging our tutors to create these spaces, to claim space and time for their own self-reflection, we are setting up conditions under which they can learn from writers as well as teach them; and we are encouraging tutors to value the writing center as a place where both tutor and writer truly learn and grow.

When school time conflicts with learning time, we must be attentive to "the pause that refreshes" in writing conferences. Perhaps "wait time" (Mary Budd Rowe) and "think time" (Robert J. Stahl) are the needed antidotes to "seat time"—that enforced and measured fungible time that students are acculturated to by years of schooling.[5] Rowe and Stahl, teacher-researchers, found wait-time benefits for both students and teachers that extend to the writer/tutor dyad. For example, simply doubling the average wait time of 1.5 seconds after a question—waiting even three seconds for a response—elicited longer, more complex and confident answers. With additional wait time, teachers, and by extension, tutors, can experience the following outcomes:

⌧ Their questioning strategies tend to be more varied and flexible.

⌧ They decrease the quantity and increase the quality and variety of their questions.

⌧ They ask additional questions that require more complex information processing and higher-level thinking on the part of students. (Stahl)

Our cultural impulse to fill gaps in dialogue makes us fear that time without talk is time wasted. A powerful meme, for example, is that time is money. As Levine says, "If you believe time is money, waiting is . . . expensive" (101). In Levine's chapter describing ten rules that are "part of the silent language of culture" (102), his rule nine states, "Time can be given as a gift" (123). Just as Lewis Hyde waxes eloquent on gifting, Levine writes, "The 'offering' of time is notable because it goes beyond an explanation of profit and gain or supply and demand" (124). We're not sure we believe anymore in time-wasting as a concept, or at least not as a negative concept. Certainly we no longer believe silence maps so readily to wasted time. We think maybe our assumptions about silence prevent us from seeing its power.

IMAGINING THE FUTURE, ALREADY HERE

The five of us have become fascinated with what organizational management types call "future perfect thinking." What could be better for us in writing centers than a vision of time that relies on a knowledge of verb tenses? Put simply, studies have shown that when we imagine our futures in the future tense, we're unlikely to be able to fill in the details of what will happen in the future. But when we imagine the future as something that has already happened, we are more able to fill in the details of what will have happened. Tricky, huh? But again and again in research, those asked to describe a car accident, a football game, or the itinerary of a professor who took a sabbatical, in the future perfect tense, offer more detail and fewer generalities (Bavelas, Webb and Watzke, and Weick, in Weick 195–199). Karl Weick explains the phenomena this way: "When one imagines the steps in a history that will realize an outcome, then there is more likelihood that one or more of the steps will have been performed before and will evoke past experiences that are similar to the experience that is imagined in the future perfect tense. When the past is imported into the present, resemblances are noted; the future is put into one kind of context, and thereby becomes more familiar and meaningful" (Weick 198). (Notice how this same idea reappears in Donald

Schön and Malcolm Gladwell's thinking, which we consider in the next chapter.) As Weick says, with future perfect thinking, "There is less of a question about whether my current efforts are sensible . . . and I am simply going about the business of producing that uneventful, inevitable outcome" (198–199).

Write a letter of congratulations to yourself for all you've accomplished, Weick suggests, when you can't write the five-year plan you have been assigned. Play with "utilitarian daydreaming" and write "a fan letter you would like to receive, a review of your unfinished work, a prophetic autobiography covering events starting tomorrow and going for a year, or even an obituary" (199). How might these mischievously self-congratulatory bits of writing invite trickster and all attendant possibilities into our sense of what we feel we'll never accomplish, we wonder?

As much as thinking *about the future* can seem open to possibility, it can give way to assumptions and paranoia. If you imagine, as a director, "They will move my writing center! And just when I am settled in the new space, I know they will want to move me again!" What if, engaging in future perfect thinking, a director were to imagine "The writing center will have moved into the new space, and in that space, the writing center will have become the premier learning environment on campus"? So we need to ask ourselves as we exercise future perfect thinking: what will it take for this to happen? This kind of thinking is not grand illusion or fantasy—it can actually help us deal with unknowns:

> The simple future tense is a difficult tense to work with because any possible outcome might occur. Future perfect thinking, on the other hand, can make speculation more manageable by focusing on single events. If an event is projected and thought of as already accomplished, it can be more easily analyzed. (Weick 199)

For us, this future perfect thinking is also intimately related to the functional leadership we wrote about in our introduction and in following chapters. To accomplish institutional transformation, it may be that we have to imagine what it would look like once institutional transformation has already taken place. We may need to imagine that we will have accomplished all we will have hoped to accomplish—even if we will have felt as if we hardly had the time to do all we needed to do it.

4

ORIGAMI, ANYONE?
Tutors as Learners

Since there are no final agreements, teachers and students should simply learn to love the questions.

Maxine Greene

A chapter on tutors as learners may, at this point, seem redundant, since we try throughout this book to highlight the ways in which we are all learning all the time as we engage in our work. Nevertheless, this chapter is designed to highlight the need for a mindfulness to the work of teaching in a writing center environment and to call for an attention to functional leadership that can result in rich communities of practice. While we may assume that writing centers need little defending as sites for learning on our campuses, promoting the kind of learning environment we are writing about does, we believe, need defending. As we indicated earlier, we aren't advocating traveling practices, but a way of looking at learning and leadership that is really an almost invisible weaving of practice and theory, for as Etienne Wenger points out, there is "no dichotomy between the practical and the theoretical, ideals and reality, or talking and doing. Communities of practice include all of these" (48).

Even working from the basic premise that students attending our schools are learners, we have to account for the kind of learning, the learning culture, if you will, that a writing center could provide. Imagine the faculty, professional staff, graduate students and undergraduates in your centers: they do not learn in simply one environment and in one way. Writing centers can be sites for learning cultures that recognize and honor the multiple ways we work not just from *what we already know,* but from what we are learning in the moment. We want to remember to be surprised by the everyday, to see with different eyes. In trying to devise ways to support these goals through our staff education, we want to design activities and intellectual challenges that get tutors to look at their everyday experiences differently. We want our tutors to step around or step outside of how they usually see. We want them to see connections. We want to do the same ourselves.

In the Trickster chapter, we discussed the problems of viewing writing center theory and practice through the lens of what Donald Schön terms "technical rationality" (3). We encouraged recognizing and valuing the artistry, the ways of knowing, becoming, and practicing in a writing center. In the present chapter we will explore what teaching and learning might look like in a writing center that embraces the practices associated with a learning culture.

Our job as writing center directors is to support that learning culture for tutors, thus empowering them to support a learning culture for the writers they meet. We want our tutors to learn with and from their work, both their triumphs and their mistakes. In this chapter, we will point to a variety of possibilities for fostering such conditions, but offer no iron-clad, step-by-step road map. This is dynamic work. Many times we find ourselves learning as we go. Working in these ways may leave tutors—and us—less settled, admittedly, but also more poised for learning at the point of need. The approaches we suggest are complementary, *and* they are potentially irreconcilable. What we mean is that moving through these approaches is non-linear, not reduced to the well-worn path of taking novice to expert. When we five think about tutors' learning, we come at it from a variety of angles, just as we want tutors to be able to enter conferences from a variety of angles.

CREATING A CULTURE OF LEARNING

Unfortunately, most educational institutions still follow what Peter Senge, and other organizational leadership theorists, call the Industrial-Age model, one that values schools "run by specialists who maintain control," where tasks "are broken into discrete pieces called 'jobs' filled by teachers, principals, superintendents, and school boards" (*Schools That Learn* 43). Ah, you might say, but isn't that efficient? If we're looking for what John Tagg terms "structural leadership" (338), the kind that's defined largely as maintaining a place-holding job, perhaps so. The status quo is maintained, but at what price? Senge goes on: "It is assumed that if each person does his or her highly specialized job, then things will work out," when in reality everyone works in isolation. There is very little partnership, very little teamwork (43). Knowledge is atomized into manageable chunks—history, math, English—and students experience "a highly fragmented system that is the antithesis of a team" (43). What we're advocating here is certainly teamwork, but much more than that. We are advocating what Tagg calls "functional leadership," the kind that goes beyond the mere structural to embrace and value not only the mission and purpose of the work but the diversity of others' experiences as well (338). This is the kind of leadership that escapes from the rigidity of hierarchies and the fear of failure. Developing and assessing a culture of leadership and learning is a recursive process, a process all of us try to build into the everyday of our centers. We found it useful to turn to people outside of our own writing center/composition circles, to find tools that would help us think deeply about leadership and learning.

We offer Marcia Connor's Learning Audit,[1] originally designed for business managers. (See table 1 on facing page.) The questions on this audit have led us to hear the questions that writing center directors pose to one another, with new ears. How might we respond to the idea of awards for tutors if, for example, we were to think about the questions that put "senior management bonuses" on a spectrum with "energy comes in large part from learning and growing"? How might we answer the question of whether tutors should have downtime if we honored how necessary reflecting on "what has happened and what may happen" is to a pro-learning culture?

In fact, Connor's audit inspired us to design one of our own as a device to help us focus this book. We are not suggesting that anyone would set out to create what Connor calls an "anti-learning culture," and we do realize that we've artificially constructed binaries here. But we know how tempting it is to be efficient with our time, to take short cuts by making unilateral decisions. The chart we offer as Table 2 has helped us to see how we might inadvertently fall into some anti-learning practices. It is by no means comprehensive, and we invite you to design your own if you, like us, are interested in assessing your work this way. (See page 52.)

While writing this audit and this chapter, we turned once more to the work of Etienne Wenger to help us articulate the issues we've been wrestling with—primarily how to explain the kind of culture we're advocating. As teachers and directors, we all want tutors who are actively engaged in their work, and Wenger offers guidance here. A viable community of practice, he tells us, consists of a group of diverse people who make meaning together by sharing their experiences and who learn from one another so that no one is expected to know everything about the practice: "From this perspective, *communities of practice can be thought of as shared histories of learning*" (86). Such a group is able to talk about the ways that their individual and collective abilities have changed, and in doing so, they rely on "the shared historical resources, frameworks, and perspectives that can sustain mutual engagement in action" (5). Finally, members can see the impact of the learning community on their

TABLE 1

Conner's Learning Audit

PRO-LEARNING CULTURE	1-5	ANTI-LEARNING CULTURE	1-5
People at all levels ask questions and share stories about successes, failures, and what they have learned.		Managers share information on a need-to-know basis. People keep secrets and don't describe how events really happened.	
Everyone creates, keeps, and propagates stories of individuals who have improved their own processes.		Everyone believes they know what to do, and they proceed on that assumption.	
People take at least some time to reflect on what has happened and what may happen.		Little time or attention is given to understanding lessons learned from projects.	
People are treated as complex individuals.		People are treated like objects or resources without attention to their individuality.	
Managers encourage continuous experimentation.		Employees proceed with work only when they feel certain of the outcome.	
People are hired and promoted on the basis of their capacity for learning and adapting to new situations.		People are hired and promoted on the basis of their technical expertise as demonstrated by credentials.	
Performance reviews include and pay attention to what people have learned.		Performance reviews focus almost exclusively on what people have done.	
Senior managers participate in training programs designed for new or high-potential employees.		Senior managers appear only to "kick off" management training programs.	
Senior managers are willing to explore their underlying values, assumptions, beliefs, and expectations.		Senior managers are defensive and unwilling to explore their underlying values, assumptions, beliefs, and expectations.	
Conversations in management meetings constantly explore the values, assumptions, beliefs, and expectations underlying proposals and problems.		Conversations tend to move quickly to blaming and scapegoating with little attention to the process that led to a problem or how to avoid it in the future.	
Customer feedback is solicited, actively examined, and included in the next operational or planning cycle.		Customer feedback is not solicited and is often ignored when it comes over the transom.	
Managers presume that energy comes in large part from learning and growing.		Managers presume that energy comes from "corporate success," meaning profits and senior management bonuses.	
Managers think about their learning quotient, that is, their interest in and capacity for learning new things, and the learning quotient of their employees.		Managers think they know all they need to know and that their employees do not have the capacity to learn much.	
Total for a pro-learning culture		*Total for anti-learning culture*	

The column with the highest total represents the type of culture you have today.

own identities and find "a way of talking about how learning changes who [they] are"; they are able to create "personal histories of becoming in the context of [their] communities" (5). This is a tall order. And there's more. The participants must be included in what matters to that community (74), which implies, echoing Tagg, the kind of leadership that makes room for negotiation among all members. So how do we help new tutors to move from being outsiders to full membership within

TABLE 2
Writing Center Learning Audit

PRO-LEARNING CULTURE	1-5	ANTI-LEARNING CULTURE	1-5
Writing Center policy is always discussed/ negotiated with staff.		Writing Center policy is made by the director and then announced at staff meetings.	
Everyone is comfortable sharing stories of success and failure.		Tutors usually keep to themselves if they believe a session has gone badly. The Director only shares success stories among colleagues.	
Director and tutors frequently consult with each other when they are unsure of a course of action.		People believe they know what to do and don't see the need to consult with others.	
There's space and time to process what is being learned.		Material is presented at staff meetings and is rarely revisited.	
Experimentation is encouraged.		Tutors want and are expected to follow an acceptable format for each session.	
Tutors are hired based on their diverse life experiences and flexibility.		Tutors are hired based on their grades and faculty recommendations.	
Hiring practice and decisions are a shared responsibility.		Director does the hiring.	
Clerical and tutorial staff frequently share ideas – there is mutual learning.		There is a hierarchy between clerical and tutorial staff.	
Disagreements/tensions are discussed and processed together. Sanctions are rarely necessary.		When there is tension/dissension among the staff, the director determines who is to blame and takes appropriate action.	
Students who use the center are encouraged to give feedback including both formal and informal written and oral forms, through focus groups, and other dialogic means.		Feedback is solicited in written, post-tutorial evaluation forms only. Students who use the center show up in the demographics part of the annual report. Student feedback is summarized for external audiences only.	
Opportunities for reflection are built in to tutors' schedules as well as into staff development meetings. Tutors' reflective writing is encouraged and valued.		Tutors are scheduled in sessions for every hour they work.	
Together, directors and tutors explore underlying assumptions about the theoretical underpinnings of their practice.		Tutors and the director are most interested in leaving theory outside the writing center – the work is focused on strategies.	
Tutors bring in readings that interest them, which are then incorporated into the course.		Directors determine the readings and activities included in staff preparation courses.	
Annual reports get to the real work of the center and are designed to be useful to current and future tutors.		Annual reports are primarily quantitative in nature and written exclusively for an external audience.	
Issues regarding race, gender, sexual orientation, ethnicity, and/or religion are addressed both personally and in staff meetings in ways that explore values, assumptions, beliefs, and expectations.		Because issues such as race, gender, sexual orientation, ethnicity and/or religion are touchy, they are rarely, if ever, discussed personally or in staff meetings.	
Tutors plan staff education meetings or collaborate with the Director in planning.		The Director plans all staff education meetings or approves plans of tutors for staff education.	
Directors demonstrate active learning along with the staff.		Directors make and grade assignments, but do not participate in fulfilling them.	
Tutors receive raises based upon their engagement in the learning community.		Tutors receive raises based upon years of service.	
Tutors and the director participate in exploring new ways of learning.		Tutors and the director prefer to stay with familiar academic discourse.	
Tutors and the director are involved in regional and national organizations (i.e. through reading and discussion of WLN, WCJ, C's and/ or participation at professional conferences).		Tutors and the director do not have the time or resources to participate.	
Tutor participation in regional and national conferences is encouraged, supported, and valued.		Director participates in regional and national conferences as presenter/facilitator, but tutors do not.	
Conference preparation is organized and executed by the director and the staff.		Conference preparation is organized and executed by the director.	
Total for Pro-Learning Culture		*Total for Anti-learning culture*	

the learning culture? We involve them in learning in practice, as Wenger suggests:

> *Evolving forms of mutual engagement:* discovering how to engage, what helps and what hinders; developing mutual relationships; defining identities. . . .
>
> *Understanding and tuning their enterprise:* aligning their engagement with it, and learning to become and hold each other accountable to it; struggling to define the enterprise and reconciling conflicting interpretations of what the enterprise is about.
>
> *Developing their repertoire, styles, and discourses:* renegotiating the meaning of various elements; producing or adopting tools, artifacts, representations; recording and recalling events; inventing new terms and redefining or abandoning old ones; telling and retelling stories; creating and breaking routines. (95).

These three elements, we suggest, offer an alternate rubric for a Ready-Set-Go staff education method, replacing a more strategy-driven staff preparation sequence. We use these elements as touchstones throughout this and the following chapters.

READY? IDENTITIES IN MOTION

One of our first priorities is to actively recruit a diverse staff to provide a fertile ground for the making of meaning. We will talk more about this in chapter six, but it is important to consider here as well. It may mean rethinking how and where you look for new tutors. For example, many of us look to honors classes. But what do these classes look like? Is everyone of traditional college age? Are the majority of the students white? Are most middle class? Do most speak English as a first language? We're not saying that honors students do not make good tutors, but we are saying that, at many universities, honors programs are structured in such a way as to preclude non-traditional students and talented students of color from participation.[2] Perhaps you belong to a diversity committee, or have a colleague who works with returning students, or you know the advisor to the gay/lesbian group, or know of a way to find students who have struggled with basic writing before gaining competence in their majors. Think of the resources we have in our own lives that may help us to add depth to our staffs. Recruiting and maintaining a diverse staff is difficult and, at times, may lead to conflict. Shared belief, though, for Wenger, isn't a requirement here, nor is agreement among staff members, and when problems arise, they are rich in possibility, "occasions for the production of new meanings" (84). Think, for example, of what new directions a discussion of literacy might take in your staff education course when you have tutors who speak Spanish at home, or when one of your tutors reveals his anger when his two home languages—Creole and Black English—are obliterated by "standard" English. Or how about the single, working mother who identifies with bell hooks's discussion of the impact class and race has on learning and brings her own graphic experiences to what was a safe predictable, schooled discussion? Think of how these conversations may impact tutoring and learning.

Once staff is selected and we make room for the voices of those who had not previously been included and create conditions in which those voices may be heard and respected, our writing centers can be transformed by new perspectives, new frames. In order to initiate and maintain engagement in writing center practice richly conceived, however, there must be constant negotiation among all participants and careful attention to providing spaces where individual learning can be shared, where experiences can be honored. We recognize, with Schön, that:

> [w]hen a practitioner sets a problem, he chooses and names the things he will notice . . . Through complementary acts of naming and framing, the practitioner selects things for attention and organizes them, guided by an appreciation of the situation that gives it coherence and sets a direction for action. (4)

All of the dynamics of life experience, education, identity, political and economic position and affiliation, Schön tells us, inform the ways in which any one of us may name and frame problems. When we come together in a writing center, we bring with us those naming and framing practices in which we have been schooled as well as those we have cultivated based on lived experience. We want to recognize the ways in which the varying frames tutors (and directors) bring to the writing center may conflict. Rather than suppressing those conflicts, we are inclined to recognize them as intriguing phenomena and as dynamics rich with meaning-making potential. We recognize that creating and sustaining a learning culture means we must make conscious, explicit, and accessible to inquiry those naming and framing practices we and our tutors bring to our work.

The five of us have noticed with astonishing regularity the degree to which the frames in which we have been schooled and which we see scripted into established, traditional writing center practice fail in the actual encounter between tutor and writer. We have also noticed that occasionally a tutor (or two or three or four) seem exceptionally competent even, or perhaps especially, in circumstances that defy accepted practice and policy. Rather than putting those instances down to individual talent or exceptional intuition, we have begun to wonder about them and to design tutor education around "what we can learn from a careful examination of artistry, that is, the competence by which practitioners actually handle indeterminate zones of practice" (Schön13). In tutor education both inside and outside of the classroom, we want to create opportunities for tutors to turn that habit of naming and framing on its head, as it were. We want tutors to see themselves, the writers with whom they work, and the complex and dynamic conditions within tutorials through Coyote eyes—not as old problems with fixed solutions, but as moments of intrigue and as opportunities for wonderment and becoming.

Each of us—writers, tutors, directors—enters the writing center with many pasts, at least one present, and numerous possible futures. We each think about our own writing history and we think about other writers' histories. We ponder whether and when tutors are "ready" to tutor. We wonder if our institutions will ever acknowledge our work, our successes, or our visions. Finally, we've realized that arching over all of these questions is the necessity of returning again and again in our thinking to the relationship of the past, present and future.

For Wenger, within communities of practice, "[t]he work of identity is always going on" (154), and though "issues of identity as a focus of overt concern may become more salient at certain times than at others, our identity is something we constantly renegotiate during the course of our lives" (154). Though we might commonly think of identities as made up of our past selves brought to bear on present moments, Wenger suggests otherwise. Neither the past nor the future is set in stone. As a result, identities, both individual and collective, are in constant motion; a community of practice "is a field of possible pasts and of possible futures, which are all there for participants, not only to witness, hear about, and contemplate, but to engage with" (Wenger 156).

Therefore, as Wenger writes:

> The temporality of identity in practice is thus a subtle form of temporality. It is neither merely individual nor simply linear. The past, the present, and the future are not in a simple straight line, but embodied in interlocked trajectories. It is a social form of temporality, where the past and the future interact as the history of a community unfolds across generations. (158)

To us, Wenger's explanations are integral to considering the potential of returning tutors and new tutors, returning writers and writers new
to the writing center and the ongoing cultivation of a learning culture.
We can all recognize, for example, that newcomers to any group may
have their understandings of their identities challenged as new ideas
and experiences disrupt old ways of being and knowing, but we might
forget that old-timers can be newcomers too—when they encounter
readings or situations that challenge them anew. Drawing on Wenger, we
try to work with tutors to *get lost*, rather than to feel as though they've lost
some thing, as Rebecca Solnit frames that distinction. When we lose something, Solnit tells us, "everything is familiar except that there is one item
less, one missing element" (22). But when we allow ourselves to *get lost*,
"the world has become larger than our knowledge of it" (22). The question for Solnit is not whether "you can know the unknown," but "how to
go about looking for it, how to travel" (24). The reification promoted by
lock-step or strategy-driven practice too often, in our experience, results
in tutors who feel as though they have lost some thing: "That session
would have gone better if I had read that poem, if the student had had
a copy of the assignment, if our *MLA Handbook* weren't MIA. If. If. If."
When we help our tutors to get lost, we open them to possibilities in the
ways that Wenger suggests, and, by extension, they can encourage writers to get lost (in the best sense of that term) as well.

One of our favorite staff meeting activities grew out of just this sense
of getting lost, as we poked around on the writing center staff computer,
looking to see what bookmarks the tutors had added. We clicked on the
newly-bookmarked link for a daily horoscope site and began to plan the
first meeting of the year, one at which we wanted new tutors to articulate
their anxieties about beginning their writing center work. We passed
around descriptions of the various astrological signs and asked tutors to
write their writing center horoscopes. While we certainly could have simply asked tutors to freewrite on some of their initial concerns, this slight
modification led to some unexpected revelations and reinforced the
importance of flexibility and creativity in engaging in this job. We advocate remaining open to such everyday moments, not simply to introduce
newcomers, but to help all tutors envision their future selves as full participants in the community. Think about these everyday moments, build
on what tutors suggest to you, through writing, conversation, magnetic
poetry, Internet bookmarks. Those opportunities open up ways to talk
about practice, to negotiate shared meanings, to develop a repertoire.

Late in the semester, when we recognize the need to acknowledge pressures and frustrations, yet we want to avoid a meeting that turns into a gripe session, we still turn to the tutors' everyday experiences, this time to consider how we might challenge our identities in ways that allow them to let off a little steam while also opening doors to richer considerations of practice. We have asked them, for example, to work in groups to come up with a Writing Center Superhero, complete with superpowers. What does your group's superpower suggest about what you are finding frustrating or difficult about the ways you are expected to work, we ask. A writing center mascot, Tutorious Rex, began his tenure in the writing center as a character in one of these Writing Center Superhero skits. On the Magna Doodle, Tutorious Rex was brought to life, pounding through town like Godzilla and chomping through books at the local library. His superpower? To gain knowledge by literally consuming it. In the conversations that followed, we "read" the drawing of Tutorious, discussing how this superpower might be used for good as well as for evil, problematizing the idea of consumption of information and the pressures tutors feel, in our generalist writing centers, to know not only about writing but also about Heidegger's *Being and Time* or string theory. Several days later, a plastic dinosaur made an appearance on the main tutoring table, a gift from one of the tutors, and named, of course, Tutorious. When she had a bit of downtime one afternoon, Sally, the tutor who had found Tutorious on the shelf of a local toy store, took some construction paper and made some tiny books to fit in his mouth. Tutorious functioned as a release valve during the stressful days of nonstop tutoring, and it was not uncommon for us to find our Mr. Incredible action figure and Tutorious joining forces to throw off the oppression of the *MLA Handbook*. Once, we nearly stumbled over Lauren, our resident photographer-tutor, crouched down near the Writing Center's door, shooting Tutorious as he slouched toward a session—a shot that wound up on the cover of our Writing Center Theme-Song CD (entitled "Chomp: Jammin' With Tutorious").

Much emphasis has been placed on what directors believe students need in order to feel comfortable in our writing centers. Like Nancy Grimm, Jackie Grutsch McKinney and others, we do not proceed, necessarily, from an assumption of comfort, nor would we presume to know, really, what, if anything, would make everyone comfortable. The activities we have described in this chapter, like the horoscope activity and the Writing Center Superhero activity, are designed, in many ways, to help our tutors feel comfortable with intellectual discomfort, to encourage a speculative, exploratory mindset. As directors, we too must speculate and explore, and, while we may be limited in our abilities to ascertain what our very diverse student populations need to do their best work (though it is certainly our job to try our hardest to do so), the five of us have become quite skilled at reading what our tutors need to do *their* best work. We have learned that what the tutors need may not always be what we expect. Certainly these needs don't line up neatly with what Jackie Grutsch McKinney calls the "iconic" writing center must-haves: couches, plants, and coffee pots.

In "Leaving Home Sweet Home: Towards Critical Readings of Writing Center Spaces," McKinney critiques writing center efforts to create "homey" spaces, arguing that our models of home are marked by class, by race, by gender (among other things) in ways that make these spaces more homey for some than for others. She wonders whether students are as interested in the space as they are in the work, and she suggests that we have not accurately assessed what factors bring students to the writing center and what factors lead them to return. She writes, "In an effort to get more students to use their services, writing centers may unwittingly be putting too much emphasis on the affective dimension of tutoring instead of on the intellectual. We shortchange our students if we doubt that they are interested in serious intellectual conversations" (18). We agree with McKinney, and look for the serious intellectual opportunities in what might otherwise seem like the least serious moments, such as in our work with Tutorious Rex.

McKinney observes that "what gets used most in [her] writing center, what is indeed indispensable . . . are computers, Kleenex, a stapler, cleaning spray, pencils, trash cans, breath mints, bulletin boards, our telephone, forms, the front desk, a coat rack, and our worn copies of the *Everyday Writer* handbook" (18). Rather than evoking *another* place (i. e., home), such items evoke *this* place, which should really be our goal, argues McKinney. "We can begin to listen to our centers if we look *at* our spaces as opposed to *through* them," she concludes (18).

We look around our writing centers. Where are our tutors expressing themselves? Do the items available to our tutors resonate with them? Several of us, for example, have lots of space available, so large rolls of white paper and various markers are always around. Doodles scrawled at the beginning of the semester turn into full-fledged art projects by the end. Others of us don't have much room to launch big projects, so the markers and paper tend to lay fallow, but the out-of-the-way items—the magnetic poetry, Magna Doodles, and screensavers—are always revealing, as are the pages the tutors print on the writing center printer and leave behind, the notes tutors leave for one another, and the resource books left un-shelved.

Seeing the everyday in these artifacts is one way to uncover what means and what matters in our writing centers.

SUSTAINING A CULTURE OF LEARNING

If we are to create and sustain learning cultures within our writing centers, we will need to consider carefully how we and our tutors frame the work of teaching writing. In his book *Writing/Teaching: Essays Toward a Rhetoric of Pedagogy*, Paul Kameen examines and critiques the way the pedagogical transaction between teacher and student has often been framed. An over-determined sense of teacher authority, Kameen argues, leads to a transmission-of-knowledge model that displaces the possibility of mutual learning—students and teachers being changed in and through the production of knowledge within a teaching/learning encounter. Kameen suggests that a binary between research and teaching that now prevails in the current organizing logic of higher education forces us to conceive of teaching as the performance of *being*, rather than of *becoming*, knowledgeable. Inadvertently, what we teach tutors when we, even tacitly, subscribe to the binary that "Teaching is not-research. Research is not-teaching" is that they must have expertise, claim authority, and resist being changed by or learning in their interactions with writers (170). If we are able to cultivate in ourselves and in our tutors an awareness of teaching as learning, as *becoming* rather than as a display of *being* knowledgeable, we will be well on our way to creating a sustainable learning culture within our writing centers.

To engage a pedagogy of becoming, we will need to keep in mind what we know students can learn, value, and take away from their experiences and work to develop an extra-curriculum of activities that will combine to help tutors discover how to engage with each other and the writers they'll be working with. When we do this, we escape the constraints of a narrow vision of "tutor training."

It seems to us, then, that staff education projects should always:

- help students make connections between what they already know they know, what they know but don't know they know, and what they don't yet know
- disrupt certainty and surprise participants with unexpected insights
- pose learning as always "becoming," not just "being" (Kameen 126, 127, 173–174)

- show that teachers can be learners and learners can be teachers; everyone is, in fact, an ongoing learner and a developing teacher, no matter their profession, current or future

What we suggest applies whether tutors are faculty, professional, undergrads, grads, or volunteers—or any crazy combination you can think of—because when there is a learning culture and all members teach and learn from where they are, there need not be such divisions.

Most of our tutors, from undergraduates to professionals, are people who have learned to "do school" well. They know what they need to do to get the grade, to achieve the certification that translates into one degree of expertise or another. We are committed, however, to helping them move toward what John Tagg calls an incremental theory of learning. An awareness that, as tutors accumulate and share experiences in the writing center, they will begin to make meaning together and prepare for mutual engagement in the community leads us to slow down their cognitive processes a bit whenever we can, subject them to scrutiny, and disrupt the commodification of knowledge that can follow from perceived expertise. One way to unsettle this march toward mastery is by working with tutors to access and maintain what Sheryl Fontaine has called "the beginner's mind" (208). When Fontaine, who teaches and directs a writing center, begins karate lessons, she realizes what expertise in her career causes her to miss in the everyday. With karate she starts to notice life around her through her new "beginner's mind," and she writes: "Without the cavalier familiarity of the expert, without the monotony of well-known situations, my beginner's mind has been forced to reach toward a felt sense, a point inside of me from which I focus on the process of doing karate and on each moment of that doing" (209).

In our writing centers, we have designed and refined learning projects geared toward the beginner's mind. Hanging out in the center while tutors are working on these projects, visitors might overhear an exchange that goes something like this:

Nikki: Where the hell are the wire cutters?
Lisa: Hey, who's got the French wires?
Graham: How am I supposed to get this thing twisted around? ARRRGGHHH! I broke the eye pin!

The tutors on this occasion are learning to make earrings—not as a way to enhance the budget (but, hey, there's an idea . . .), but as one more demonstration of how we teach and learn. In this case, the tutors not only learn something new themselves, they also teach it to the others using a variety of methods. This year, Missy has taught a fellow tutor to make earrings, and now that tutor is teaching everyone else.

As the projects help everyone remember how it feels to start again, they also remind us of how much we actually bring to new experiences. Graham has trouble manipulating the small tools, but he has some expertise in buying jewelry for his girlfriend. Lisa is an art major with a sophisticated sense of design. Nikki—although preferring to buy her signature long, dangly earrings—has a flair for the dramatic in her creations. In the room are both laughter and frustration.

For several years now, we, along with our tutors, have learned how to root plants, make clay pigs, fashion balloon animals, cook a four-course meal, make paper, and do ikebana and origami. Surprises abound, with some bonus value-added, oh-wow sorts of insights and unanticipated doorways to new places.

Knitting, currently in vogue, is a perennial favorite project among the tutors. After one particular knitting demonstration during which everyone was all arms, needles, and dropped stitches, several of the tutors formed a knitting group. During the cold winter months, they produced miles of scarves and one sweater. All that stitchery took place in the tutor lounge, right along with conversations about politics, tutoring, classes, and personal problems—almost like writing around one of Gere's kitchen tables. How important are these moments to writing and writing center work?

An answer to that question, it seems to us, lies within Linda Brodkey's essay, "Writing on the Bias." In that piece, Brodkey explores her working class roots and a collage of experiences to discover the influences on her writing and teaching. She describes her mother's passion for sewing and for cutting fabric on the bias to ensure that the garment "hang right" as a central influence on her development as a writer. She says,

> If I enjoy the labor of writing, that can at least in part be explained by my writing as my mother sewed. She made clothes. I make prose. There is a sense in which just as my mother was always sewing, I am always writing . . . and none of us knows when we are talking if we are just talking—or writing—or sewing. (545–546)

So are the tutors knitting, talking, writing, tutoring? We would say all of the above, and the sense that tutors are always teaching one another and learning from one another is something we want to instill, something that is essential to a learning community, a community of practice. Think of the vegetarian recipes exchanged and the dissertation formatting advice that travels among a staff. Is that learning? We think so.

We would not be doing the learning projects justice, however, if we portrayed them as only producing cozy pictures of Zen-like downtime. Sometimes they are boring and uninspired (a good reminder of what teaching and learning are like when boring and uninspired?). Other times, they shake things up, throw us Trickster curve balls, like this one: the learning project was to use clicker training to teach a twelve-hundred pound pet horse to throw a hula hoop over his head. Central to the teaching-to-the-tutors component of the project was the "The Clicker Game," devised by Karen Pryor (1999), an activity relying solely on kinetic learning, an approach that was not the preferred learning style of most of the tutors.

To play the clicker game, one person (the subject) leaves the room while the rest of the group determines a task for the "trainer" to help the subject perform. The subject, in this case, was to go to the coat rack, take down an umbrella, and open it. The rub is that no language is used; instead, a clicker sounds whenever the subject makes a move in the right direction. Usually, the game is fun, with lots of laughter and success. This time, however, the tutor-as-subject had unusual difficulty "reading" the situation, since learning this way was incredibly alien to her. Finally she became so frustrated that she began to cry.

The game was ended, and the rest of the meeting was spent revisiting what it means to have the beginner's mind when everyone else seems to "get it." What must it feel like to be two days off the plane from China? What is it like to be a student with dysgraphia faced with a writing assignment? How does it feel to be the first in your family to go to college? This experience was also a reminder that tutors, especially, are students accustomed to "getting it," and they sometimes have little patience with themselves (and others) when success doesn't come as quickly or as easily as they would like.

Shaking up our worlds by revisiting that beginner's mind helps us to be present for the many writers who enter our centers, crossing that threshold into the academic house of mirrors otherwise known as a Burkean Parlor. At the very least, the recognition of a tutor's discomfort and the reasons behind it provide a space to reflect on what it is like to always be a learner, as Fontaine acknowledges: "I now understand through experience what I used to understand mostly through intellect: It's the doing that makes us 'get used to it,' that makes the conventions uncomfortably visible before they become transparent with familiarity" (211).

THE GOOD, THE BAD, AND THE UGLY: REIFICATION

Learning projects like the ones we've described above cannot alone provide the scaffolding necessary for tutors to reflect both in action and on action (Schön 26). Tutors must also, as Wenger points out, share "historical and social resources, frameworks, and perspectives" (5) in order to be fully engaged. In other words, tutors and directors need to turn to perspectives and frames that become part of the ground for a common repertoire. We advocate here the kind of reification that Wenger defines broadly as "abstractions, tools, symbols, stories, terms, and concepts that reify something of that practice in congealed form" (59). In this sense, the written texts of learning projects, for example, and even the scarves produced by tutor knitters represent such reifications, because they are the concrete evidence of a practice that honors the mutuality of teaching and learning. When we employ more conventional reification, texts, we must be careful to ensure that they don't preclude that mutuality. We turn again to Wenger to clarify what we lose if we depend only on these texts as the basis of our learning cultures:

> To the extent that knowledge is reified, decontextualized, or procedurized, learning can lead to a literal dependence on the reification of the subject matter, and thus . . . to a brittle kind of understanding with very narrow applicability. This is especially true if the delivery of codified knowledge takes place away from actual practice, with a focus on instructional structure and pedagogical authority that discourages negotiation. (265)

Bear with us for a moment while we try to explain. In general, tutor manuals encourage tutors to chunk their experiences and their interactions. In fact, they are usually fine examples of the type of Industrial-Age schooling to which Senge refers. Chunking necessarily, and unfortunately, attempts to lump what we five believe is a realistic assortment of tutoring opportunities into categories of problems to be dealt with. Although this is an egregious example, consider one "tutor training manual"[3] we found on the World Wide Web; the table of contents reveals that whole chapters are devoted to the following topics:

The Clueless Student
The Unfocused Student
The Disorganized Student

The Underdeveloped Student
The Unrevised Student
The Unpolished Student

What these topics suggest is that new tutors develop their knowledge base through a deficit model of instruction and not through authentic experiences and reflection or guided refinement. Other training texts provide lock-step models for starting, running, and ending a session. As Boquet argues in *Noise from the Writing Center*, this approach results in a version of the five-paragraph essay for writing center sessions—rote, repetitive, with little room for fresh insights or complicated connections. The result? The Holy Trinity of Tutoring: The Opening, The Body, The Conclusion. Scripted manuals and prescribed behaviors eliminate the spaces for intervention, constricting vision and restricting possibilities. As Monika, one of our tutors, writes, "When the tight walls of clarity are sought, the roomy space of ambiguity is lost." *Don't, can't,* and *shouldn't* overshadow *might, could,* and *should*—judgments that can be made by responsible, creative tutors continually learning as they work and reflect on their practices.

The textbooks don't, to us, fully account for or value the range of what tutors learn as they work in writing centers and, in fact, what they bring to us when they first enter our staff preparation courses; nor do the most structured of the textbooks, the most positivistic, allow for tutors to negotiate meaning. We look, then, to introduce new tutors to our work by building on what they already know, to move toward an understanding of the community they're entering.

What each of us brings from our other communities of practice to the writing center enriches our daily work. A theater major, for example, connects his work in improvisation to tutoring, and he develops a series of staff workshops. An art student brings drawing into the tutorial and then into staff meetings. In tapping the diverse experiences of all of our tutors, by including them in this way, our staff preparation courses may take on the kind of energy that indicates the engagement we hope for.

All five of us work hard to engage our tutors in designing and implementing their own learning. Yes, we choose texts for them to read, but they also choose texts for us to read, and these are frequently included in our writing center courses. An education major brings an article about learning styles. An English major brings an essay on queer theory. Not all of the readings come from course work, though. We think here about the tutor who burst into tears after working with a student from

Liberia. He had told her the story of walking to the Ivory Coast, of seeing the slaughter, of watching his family being hacked to death in front of him. At a staff meeting, the tutors decided to do some research on Liberia and included excerpts from that work in the formal staff course. Though these examples may be more obviously related to writing center practice than knitting, origami, or clicker-training, such individual or collaborative quests still put tutors in a beginner's frame of mind, in search of what they don't know and don't yet have to know but are starting to wonder about.

These I-Search, We-Search and teacher research projects we take on with our tutors are as varied as the learning projects and are often revised organically. More than one of us allows researchable questions to grow out of weekly staff education meetings. Okay, a tutor might say, let's all think about conferences that do X this week, and come back to next week's meeting with some experiences so we can further consider what we know—or don't yet know or understand—about X. Fill in X with multilingual graduate student writing in management, or the struggles of senior honors thesis writers, or science writers. Or, fill in X with the focus on the tutor by considering conferences in which tutors felt stressed, rushed, or unknowledgeable. Ask tutors to gather experiences in which they research their own actions or those of another (When did you overhear a stressful session? When did you find yourself writing too much for the student?). Tape conferences, send each staff person to the library databases to find one article that might speak to the group's concern(s), or just ask each tutor to reflect on his or her own work—both in conference and post-conference.

Let's think about time again. In a recent commentary in the *New York Times*, a doctor noted that the hospital television series *House* may be unrealistic, but not for the reasons usually cited. What Sandeep Jauhar points to as most unrealistic is that doctors on *House* "have time to solve problems." "I have worked in teaching hospitals in New York for seven years," he writes (D5). "Over this period, I have discerned a gradual decline in the intellectual climate of these institutions" (D5). Jauhar blames this decline on doctors who are "disengaged and mentally fatigued," from seeing too many patients. "They are preoccupied with getting their work done. Interesting cases tend to generate anxiety, not excitement. Mysteries are, by and large, abhorred" (D5). We know the ever-present danger of making comparisons between writing center work and the medical profession, but we were struck by this critique of doctors as learners, and we wonder if the pressures against any professional remaining a learner—no "time or inclination" (D5) to think or read, no "time or patience to cope with uncertainty," (D5), administrative cost-cutting and administrative rules—are simply the pressures we all work against. Our challenge is not to educate tutors who are rote, routine and efficient, whose first impulse is to make smart referrals to other special-ists. Our challenge is to educate tutors so they can, just as Dr. Jauhar wishes for himself and his colleagues and his students, continually "relish the magic and mysteries" of their work (D5). So we make it our goal to relish those models and mysteries in our writing center work.

THINK FAST! THIN-SLICING ON YOUR FEET

We are aware that our tutors are often in situations where they must make split-second decisions (although not the high stakes decisions faced by the doctors), where they must, in effect, enact that "thin-slicing" idea we described in the previous chapter about time. Although Malcolm Gladwell's book is called *Blink: the Power of Thinking without Thinking*, we are cautioned that it is clearly a fiction that we actually think without thinking. What Gladwell is really describing when he positions thin slic-ing as a "critical part of rapid cognition . . . [that] refers to the ability of our unconscious to find patterns in situations and behavior based on very narrow slices of experience" (23) is the way accumulated experienc-es, reflections, and proximal development inform our actions. He notes throughout *Blink* that these snap judgments should not be written off as instinct or intuition, categories that connote luck or magic or accident. He explains, instead, that what some might describe as gut reactions, first impressions, or immediate responses are actually the product of a scaffolded expertise that draws from a knowledge bank. Thin-slicing may sound quick, but it is really timely and attuned. Gladwell even describes experts' abilities to slow down stressful moments—to break them down into component parts and create appropriate responses.

What might this look like in the writing center? Well, thin-slice this:

> A student arrives in the writing center 15 minutes before his scheduled essay exam, in search of some pointers from a tutor. What do you do? Consider your responses to the above scenario. How do you feel about the solutions you came up with? Do you even have enough information to make decisions about the situation we just put before you?

To thin-slice this scene, you would instantaneously, and somewhat unconsciously, collect your thoughts, compile information, drawing on how this situation is similar or dissimilar to one you've faced in the past, about the student's gaze, body language, vocal pitch, about your own mental readiness. We are masters, according to Gladwell, at assessing complex situations instantaneously. We recognize concerns that thin-slicing rides the edges of stereotyping, yet we know that attempts to prevent tutors from making these kinds of judgments simply reinforce, rather than expose, existing stereotypes. "Why did you choose not to work with the student who had an upcoming essay exam?" is a question that creates space for reflection and dialogue, an opportunity to expose how each tutor came to decisions. A policy (implicit or explicit) prohibiting this type of session allows a potential caricature of a procrastinating, flaky sorority sister to remain unchallenged. And, of course, we remember Bryan, our tutor from the Time chapter, who, thin-slicing this scene, might have downed his last jolt of java and replied, "Well, we'd better get crackin' then." Bryan's decision is one not every tutor would have made, but it was one he was prepared to follow through on.

The case studies in *Blink* reveal trickster-like spaces where the particulars of any moment could surprise or delight, subvert or engage, the intentions of expert professionals. As Donald Schön notes, in his work on the "artistry" of professionals (34), "there are familiar situations where the practitioner can solve the problem by routine application of facts, rules, and procedures derived from the body of professional knowledge," but there are also "unfamiliar situations where the problem is not initially clear" (34). With a "framework" that relies on expert knowledge only, Schön notes, "there is little room for professional artistry, except as a matter of style grafted onto technical expertise" (34). Like Schön (and Gladwell), we lean toward a more "constructivist view of the reality with which the practitioner deals" (36). As Schön describes it:

> Communities of practitioners are continually engaged in what Nelson Goodman (1978) calls "worldmaking. Through countless acts of attention and inattention, naming, sensemaking, boundary setting, and control, they make and maintain the worlds matched to their professional knowledge and know-how. They are in transaction with their practice worlds. (36)

Working with tutors means being continually reminded of the discord students experience as they try to balance nascent expert status in their chosen professions with their roles as teachers and learners continually "in transaction with their practice worlds." We, too, feel a conflict: We want to be educating teachers, and yet we don't want "little teachers" (Bruffee) in the writing center; we want co-learners, conscious of their interactions, listening and asking as much as they're telling. One of our graduate student tutors, for example, expressed dismay that his writing center practices were critiqued for being too "little professor" like. "But I'm planning to be a professor," he said. "I *am* a little professor." We laugh as we recount this story, but we remember this moment, like so many Trickster moments, as one that really rocked our foundations.

In "Graduate Students as Writing Tutors: Role Conflict and the Nature of Professionalization," Thomas Conroy and Neal Lerner discuss the ways in which "the roles of tutor, teacher, and student overlap and conflict around the topic of 'expert knowledge'" (129). As graduate students in the writing center, Conroy and Lerner describe being on the verge of simultaneously joining academic departments as full-fledged members and questioning the wisdom behind that choice, often taking a critical view of not just day-to-day writing center work but the position of that work in larger contexts, both practical and theoretical. Mixed with this view are personal and professional questions. They "wonder if we are doing a good job, bringing experiences as classroom teachers and neophyte scholars to our work. At the same time, we occupy positions in a university hierarchy (and, perhaps, in the larger culture) that produce a great deal of anxiety, whether related to finances, career, or time" (129). In the first half of the chapter, Lerner notes he has inhabited three roles at the same time—"tutor, teacher and student" (130)—and he quickly establishes that classroom teachers and writing center tutors are often set in opposition to one another. But, he notes that "graduate student tutors occupy a space between these two extremes, a space that does not always feel comfortable as we question the extent of our authority and the influence of our expertise" (131).

All of our students, not only graduate students, experience the potential disconnect Conroy and Lerner describe, caught, as they are, in difficult boundary positions between student and professional, between tutor and professor stances, between full-fledged members of a profession and peripheral participants in their respective communities of practice. But, again, Paul Kameen offers us what we need in order to understand how to support our graduate staff members to be learners, to be boundary workers, and that is to encourage them to embrace becoming knowledgeable over being knowledgeable. We want, as does Kameen, to turn away from, and help our tutors turn away from, "a pedagogy of display" and turn toward "a pedagogy of construction," "one in which knowledge has the prospect for being constituted mutually in the process of the interaction rather than in seclusion beforehand or afterward" (175). Think about how unfamiliar this move may be to students who are themselves mired in pedagogies of display. Consider how often students are expected to *display* their accumulating knowledge—in qualifying exams, in the LSATs, in job interviews. Whenever we have opportunities, we reflect, with our staff, on the conflicts that arise between a pedagogy of display and a pedagogy of construction. We work to encourage and cultivate their facility, ability, and willingness to be surprised and to become unsettled in those zones of indeterminacy they may encounter in the writing center. In our own growing and learning processes, we note the irreplaceable value of opportunities to discern, meditate, converse, and make meaning under conditions of relative or great uncertainty. As writing center directors, we want to sustain conditions in which tutors may risk laying aside pedagogies of display in favor of pedagogies of construction and learn and be changed by that choice. We want to broker conversations among our staff about how what we do and what we learn in the doing might be radically transformed by the de-centering shift from display to construction.

A WORD OR TWO ABOUT TIME AND IDENTITY

Much of what we've discussed in this chapter involves ways in which naming and framing practices intersect with the formation of identity, our own, our tutors', and even our writing centers'. Learning in communities of practice implies, Wenger tells us, a continual negotiation of our identities. He writes, "The temporal dimension of identity is critical. Not only do we keep negotiating our identities, but they place our engagement in practice in this temporal context. We are always simultaneously dealing with specific situations, participating in the histories of certain practices, and involved in becoming certain persons" (155). When Wenger speaks of time, however, he is not speaking of fungible time. There is no clock here; there is, simply life—life comprised of "convergent and divergent trajectories" with which our identities interact. Coherence? Only, says Wenger (as we mentioned earlier), "through time that connects the past, the present, and the future" (154). How then can we tell if we and our tutors are being changed by what we and they learn together? Many of us in writing center work have the privilege of working with members of our learning communities for two, three, or even four years—time to observe changes. We can see, for example, how staff education evolves when tutors are fully invested in its design and implementation. If we reify our practice in terms of journals, or conference papers, or collaborative research, taped tutoring sessions, or poems, or drawings, or . . . well, whatever makes sense . . . we can inquire into the changing nature of our practices, the growth of our learning cultures and their impact on us and our staff. Think of ways such an inquiry might play out in an annual report. How could we present information that, instead of reporting on how many appointments a tutor had, discussed instead the growth that person had experienced? In our own experiences, we have seen tutors who have acknowledged and worked on their own racism, on their homophobia, on their notions of who belongs in college, and, yes, on their own writing and teaching. Imagine, with some future perfect thinking, just what they might take with them downstream.[4]

INSTITUTIONALIZED SCHOOLING AND DIRECTING A LEARNING CULTURE

Everything we've suggested in this chapter relies on a writing center director's ability to develop, nurture and sustain a learning culture, and the five of us are well aware of the ways in which a thriving, messy learning culture can conflict with the values and expectations of school and schooling. As Ivan Illich notes, "The modern university has forfeited its chance to provide a simple setting for encounters which are both autonomous and anarchic, focused yet unplanned and ebullient, and has chosen instead to manage the process by which so-called research and instruction are produced" (36). *School* explicitly or implicitly values certainty and skills that have already been attained and mastered. To keep a learning culture alive in a writing center, our tutors need to understand they need not "have this all down." The five of us remind our tutors—and ourselves—that we don't need to have this all down, we don't always need to know before we experiment and explore.

This may actually be what is most difficult about sustaining a learning culture. It is not easy to admit to ourselves—or others—that we are constantly learning and that we constantly need to learn more. And yet a true learning culture discourages bluffing and fakery because it prioritizes an "interest in and capacity for learning new things" over a belief that we "do not have the capacity to learn," and it rewards us for our "capacity for learning and adapting to new situations" rather than our "technical expertise" (Connor *Learning Culture Audit*).

The more we have thought about these ideas, the more we have been struck by the ways in which some of our most familiar everyday practices shut down the space of a true learning culture. We've talked about the moment when tutor and writer sit down together. "Have you ever been here before?" the tutor might ask. "No," the writer replies. "Well," the tutor says, "here's how we work." Such an exchange limits what the writer might offer to the tutor, what the tutor might decide to offer to the writer, and what the writing center can become as a result of the imaginative offerings or re-thinkings of either writer or tutor.

Perhaps the most essential bit of advice we try to take is from a production of *The Moliere Impromptu*: "In Moliere's world of impromptu, one must always say 'yes'" (March 3, 2005). This is an allusion to an exercise actors use to ready themselves for improvisational theater. In the version of the exercise with which we are familiar, pairs of actors hand one another imaginary gifts, saying aloud exactly what the present is. No matter what the gift, the actor must exclaim "thanks" and accept it graciously. We strive to encourage our tutors—and ourselves—to stay this open, not because we should always say yes to one another or to the students we work with out of agreement or endorsement but because in saying yes, in our own heads at the very least, we keep possibilities open and thereby maintain space for dialogue and engagement and disagreement.

In a learning culture, we are not just exchanging tips or skills or advice, we are exchanging time and ideas and experiences. We choose, as Ivan Illich suggests we might, "a life of action over a life of consumption . . . engendering a life style which will enable us to be spontaneous, independent, yet related to each other, rather than maintaining a life style which only allows us to make and unmake, produce and consume" (52).

5

STRAIGHTEN UP AND FLY RIGHT:
Writers as Tutors, Tutors as Writers

Ritual involves repetition . . . but not, strictly speaking, routinization, because ritual takes place outside normal time in a "primordial world." We might say, with the anthropologist Roy Rappaport, that successful ritual arrests the passing of mundane time and returns its practitioners to an apparently eternal "now" of pure presence or pure absence, a "time out of time."

Kurt Spellmeyer

In this chapter, we build from the impromptu, from the idea of saying yes to the gift. The writers who come to our centers and the tutors who work in them bring us everyday gifts of themselves and of their communities of practice, communities where they live outside of "normal" school time (and where they experience that "eternal 'now,'" places where writing occurs in epochal time). Sitting in the office with the door closed, we don't expect a knock, but we do expect the "ding" of the instant message program as Katie logs into the writing center computer and writes, "Hey, are you in there?" She does this every Tuesday morning just as her shift is about to begin. Other tutors update Facebook profiles, leave notes for the tutors whose shifts follow, or post their poetry online. Their writerly rituals are situated in the transactional and relational. Their writing lives are filled with diverse and material literacy practices, mediated through technologies, resulting in a new sense of the public sphere. As Kathleen Yancey noted in her 2004 Conference on College Composition and Communication[1] address: "Members of a writing public have learned to write, to think together, to organize, and to act within these forums largely without instruction and, more to the point here, largely without *our* instruction" (301). And we see this too.

How do we build upon what tutors already know? How do we use tutors' everyday literacy practices to kick up some of the dirt and debris that academic writing attempts to sweep under the rug? We begin by shifting our understanding of the rhythms or rituals that punctuate our writing center days. Writers, as we know, love their rituals. A special pen, a certain hour, an old oak desk. Music, no music. Elegant writers' notebooks or sleek, sophisticated iBooks. Our cultural understanding of writerly ritual is mired in the solitary. But our experience of writerly ritual in the writing center is dynamic and interactive, more akin to Rappaport's anthropological understanding of ritual not as mindless re-enactment but as mindful engagement.

Those of us who educate tutors must be mindful as well, as we are in danger of forgetting one (at least one) powerful motivating factor that brings tutors to their work in writing centers: namely, their senses of themselves as writers. Of the currently available tutor education texts, only one (Gillespie and Lerner) addresses the issue of what draws tutors to their work. Although throughout their text Gillespie and Lerner do acknowledge that tutors might consider themselves writers, they don't pursue this line of thinking (and, by extension, don't encourage their readers to pursue it). If we really believe that tutors are writers—and we do, knowing that our tutors have in many cases richer and more varied writing lives than we ourselves do—what does that mean for them as tutors? Well, we believe their identities as writers can, will, and should influence their tutoring. And by writers we don't mean creative writing majors necessarily, but writers in the sense that everyone every day is engaged as a writer in the larger learning organization that is higher education. Wenger tells us, "The process of engaging in practice always involves the whole person, both acting and knowing at once" (47–48). He goes on to say that, "We all have our own theories and ways of understanding the world, and our communities of practice are places where we develop, negotiate, and share them" (48). We five strive to have our writing center communities of practice be places where all writers, including us and our tutors, make space for a diversity of shared experience. To that end, we encourage our tutors to bring their everyday identities to their work in the center.

When we think of our tutors as writers and talk about our tutors' writing lives, we're that much more likely to encourage them to work as writers in their writing center conferences. And when we do this foregrounding of their writing lives, we intentionally remind them that they do understand the choices writers make and they do need to (and are encouraged to) help their peers (and maybe their faculty) understand the choices writers make.

IT'S ALL A MATTER OF PERSPECTIVE

And so, a month or so into the job for the new tutors (about 75% of the staff this year), a focused freewrite for the meeting goes like this:

- "As a writer, I . . ."
- "When I tutor, I . . ."
- "The best thing that happened was . . ."
- "In my wildest dreams, . . ."

We write for five minutes on each of the prompts, which are admittedly designed to get us thinking about the boundary-crossings we are engaged in as writers who tutor and tutors who write. Did it work? Yes and no. Here's part of Sara's:

> As a writer, I think, I organize, and I obsess . . . When I tutor, I see others in similar distress. However, as one responding to their work, I can assume the role of unattached observer . . . Amidst grammar mistakes and unrefined theses, I am forced to make my own theories about organization and style more explicit. The best thing that happened was I realized how much I could change how I approach my own writing. Take my own advice . . . In my wildest dreams, I never thought tutoring would help me think critically of my own writing. The process no longer seems daunting.

Tara writes a bit more explicitly about "see[ing] little pieces of me in each of the students." Those with the strongest, most positive writerly identities tend to see these same characteristics in the students they tutor. Taryn says, "As a writer, I enjoy creating. That is not work for me. I love that my homework is to make things up . . . When I tutor, I see millions of ways to do something . . . I see curious writers." Or Theresa: "As a writer, I love passion and am enchanted by words . . . When I tutor, I see passion, motivation, eagerness, determination, and strength." To be fair, Theresa follows with "I also see flaws, laziness, imperfection, and obstinacy," tendencies Theresa later admits she sees in her own writing as well. Kara admits to explicitly looking for the things she herself values: "As a writer, I always try to make it interesting . . . When I tutor . . . I love to see originality." This type of focused freewrite goes a long way toward helping tutors articulate their own processes and how they affect their work, but activities like this may inadvertently be turning our tutors inward. These activities are ultimately about the self, stroking an ego at the expense of an/other. Not what we want from the tutors. No, no, no. We want shape-shifters, "lords of the in-between" (Hyde 6). The difference between Pablo and John: "In Cage's terms . . . Picasso's attention to accident is a way of *exploring* the self, not of *leaving* it, and therefore runs the risk of indulgence and repetition" (original emphasis, Hyde 146).

The excerpts from the focused freewrites above are Picasso-esque in their attention to the self, narcissism of epic proportions: When I tutor, I see me, me, me. But enough about me, let's talk about me! The focused freewrite was instructive in this regard. We didn't quite appreciate, until we looked at those responses, that simply moving writers into the meta-cognitive realm wasn't necessarily enough to get them thinking in the ways we needed them to think. In fact, continuing down this path of self-exploration could be counter-productive to their need to respond to a range of writers and writing, could interfere with their developing abilities to reside in the "eternal 'now'," could keep them from saying "yes" to a writer they're working with. On a larger scale, writing center practices that merely focus on the individual as he or she is at any one point in time may prevent tutors' identity formation as writers and as participants in the writing center community of practice. Identity is not static. Writing center work is not static. Because something worked once ("I always get an 'A' when I use a quotation on every page," or "Always have the student read the paper out loud at the beginning of a tutoring session"), doesn't mean that it will work every time.

Let's look at another possibility. We contrast this focused freewrite with an exercise like Melissa Goldthwaite's Perspectives Essay assignment, described in *Writing on the Edge*. The prompt reads as follows: "For this essay, you will choose a word tangentially related to writing—close enough so that you can imagine some connections, far enough to deliver interesting results. In your essay, you should explore as many angles and senses of this concept as you can come up with" (71). Goldthwaite's assignment is an example of what Barbara Babcock calls "ritual clowning." The resulting essays are, in many cases, Levi-Straussian bricolage, kaleidoscopes of sense and contradiction as "structural patterns are realized by means of bits and pieces—patterns produced by the conjunction of contingency *and* constraint" (original emphasis, Babcock 5). "The comic frame," Babcock notes, "should enable people to be *observers of themselves, while acting*. . . It considers human life as a project in 'composition,' where the poet works with the materials of social relationships. Composition, translation, also 'revision,' hence offering maximum opportunities for the resources of *criticism*" (original emphasis, 11).

Notice the different kinds of response, from the same group of tutors, when the perspectives essay is assigned. The process cracks up, opening out rather than caving in. Katie, for example, chose the word "structure" because, quite simply, she loves structure; she worships at the altar of structure. She's a thesis-at-the-end-of-the-first-paragraph, three-supporting-paragraphs-in-the-body kind of gal. She admittedly initiated unwitting writers into her cult of structure. And here, we see her acknowledging the danger of that approach. Her perspectives essay begins with a diagram, followed by this caution:

> WARNING: The following document contains vagrant abuses of the noun *structure*. The reader is warned that all pretenses of a coherent and traditional format have been abandoned. THIS IS A TEST OF THE EMERGENCY STRUCTURE SYSTEM.

A running footer appears at the bottom of each page:

> The writer relinquishes all liability to any injuries sustained by the reader during, after, or as a result of the reading of this document. By reading this document, the reader agrees to waive all rights pertaining to the abovementioned subjects in the aforementioned situations.

Her essay is playful, self-mocking, like at the top of page four, where she begins a section entitled "THESIS, THESIS, WHO'S GOT MY THESIS!?" The paragraph that follows appears in the form of a help-wanted ad:

> Applications for the position of thesis statement are being accepted at this time. The party of the first part, being the paper, is concerned that without the party of the second part, being the thesis statement, the party of the first part will lose its focus and have a tendency to birdwalk since the absence of the party of the second part . . . OH NEVER MIND!

When Katie stumbles upon the Middle English etymology of "structure," which suggests a connection to "strew," she is intrigued: "[N]ow *strew* sounds like a little more fun. I picture a big bag of confetti and some kid throwing it up in the air joyously. Unfortunately, I also picture me vacuuming it up afterwards." She admits that this observation says a lot about her.

The perspectives assignment invited Trickster to the keyboard in ways we hadn't anticipated, as Zach demonstrates when he seizes the opportunity to issue both a playful critique of the assignment's constraints and a louder condemnation of the culture of "school" writing that has inscribed him. Zach chose the word "process" for a revision of his perspectives essay, precisely because his initial drafting turned out to be such an arduous, well, process:

> Chew on this: the meat processing industry is a vital approach to get our mouths watering. Looking at meat from a nutritional point of view

proteins are its basic component. The proteins serve as motor factors in the muscles and make up their construction materials. . . . [P]roteins influence many properties of meat, the most important of which is tenderness . . . For the most delicious meat, it is necessary to consider the role of proteins in meat structure with their changes and the changes in other compounds, all occurring post mortem.

Zach goes on to discuss, in somewhat gory detail, how this all happens, until his reader interrupts him: "Zach, you're still doing it wrong. Talk about writing. Senses, baby. Senses." Zach responds, "Can you sense that I've processed that yet? Allow me to retort: the 8½ by 11 piece of white paper, less than a millimeter thick—that's the meat. The words, those Times New Roman symbols in 12 point font—those are the proteins."

This observation is followed by a brief poetic interlude entitled "it's true," right justified and appearing in italics:

> *and everytime you proofread a paper*
> *everytime you read it over*
> *everytime you do spellchecker*
> *everytime you write it over*
> *and everytime your teacher says it's not tender*
> *remember*
> *you are really*
> *a meat processor*

When Zach returns to his essay, he has this to say:

At one stomach-churning point in time being a meat processor was one of the most deadly professions on the planet. But now you can be a meat processor in your very own bedroom! . . . For just four easy payments of $33,568, you can be the most dazzling, bad-ass, grisly meat processor known to man.[2] And you'll still have all your appendages to show for it! But that's not to say you won't lose your pride along the way. Teacher-humiliation insurance is not offered with this package. But you can always settle the score at ratemyprofessor.com.

BUZZ OFF!

The Perspectives Essay helped students identify the institutional communities of practice they participate in. For us, this writing also underscores the limitations those communities have placed on us, the tutors, and the writers who come to our centers. We realize that we want to help our students avoid being caught in the meat processor (and help our tutors avoid *being* meat processors). It is for this reason that the five of us resist yet another time-honored writing center practice: None of the five of us asks faculty to talk with our writing center tutors about their expectations for any particular written assignments. You know the drill. Professor X who teaches Class Y comes to the weekly meeting and describes his or her "expectations." He or she tells fifteen bored tutors exactly how he or she believes Paper #2 should be written—content, format, structure and citation. That way, when any student from Professor X's Class Y comes to the writing center for a session dealing with Paper #2, all tutors will know exactly what to say and do in conference and will know exactly what is missing from this particular student's Paper #2. No tutor will be at a loss in conference. No tutor will be confused about the genre expected. Tutors will, in fact, be nearly interchangeable. Every tutor can help every writer no matter what the tutor's or the student's major. Every writer will get what she or he needs to complete Paper #2 in a satisfactory way. No surprises for writer, tutor or, best of all, faculty. (And if the paper fails, the tutor is now at least partly to blame.) This is efficient use of writing center conference time, tradition tells us, and an efficient use of tutor-time. We don't think so.

This scenario poses more complications than we could possibly address—the student hasn't been to class; a tutor missed that particular meeting; the professor was feeling generous during her office hours one day (after she met with the writing center staff) and agreed to allow this one particular student to write her paper slightly differently from everyone else, but now the student is confused; and so on and so on, *ad nauseum*. But what we want to point out is very simple: When tutors are asked to work in this way, they cannot work from their (ever-changing) experiences as writers, and they simply encourage the writers they work with to write within strictly prescribed boundaries. Even more than that, the tutors experience repetition in the worst way—as rote, meaningless exercise, as boredom—rather than experiencing repetition as an opportunity for presence and attunement.

Yet fostering a learning culture for tutors and writers that enables them to work in attunement with their varied experiences and to pay attention to the "now" is indeed risky business. Many of them may not want to be as present as this model requires them to be. Our tutors are quite often our best students, with all the cultural baggage a devotion to schooling has entailed. Yet, they don't quite trust their own writerly advice, and, let's be honest, sometimes neither do we.

In a 1993 piece in the *New York Times Book Review*, Patricia Nelson Limerick retells a portion of a Larry McMurtry essay so she can express the "difficulty of persuading people to break out of habits of timidity, caution and unnecessary fear." McMurtry describes traveling to Texas to watch moviemakers as they adapt his novel, *Horseman, Pass By*, to film. He is, Limerick tells us, "particularly anxious to learn how the buzzard scene had gone." She writes, "In that scene, Paul Newman was supposed to ride up and discover a dead cow, look up at a tree branch lined with buzzards, and, in his distress over the loss of the cow, fire his gun at one of the buzzards. At that moment, all of the other buzzards were supposed to fly away into the blue Panhandle sky." The film makers' challenge, it seems, was to figure out both how to get the buzzards to sit still on the branch and then to figure out how, on cue, to get those same buzzards to fly off. Their initial solution was to wire the buzzards' feet "to the branch, and then . . . [after the shot] pull the wire, releasing their feet, thus allowing them to take off." This approach, however, does not account for what McMurtry came to call the "mentality of buzzards." Limerick reports, "With their feet wired, the buzzards did not have enough mobility to fly. But they did have enough mobility to pitch forward. So that's what they did: with their feet wired, they tried to fly, pitched forward and hung upside down from the dead branch, with their wings flapping."

One detail never made it into McMurtry's essay—namely that the buzzard circulatory system does not work upside down, and so, after a moment or two of flapping, the buzzards passed out—a fact that's key to Limerick's point about learned helplessness and academic writing:

> After six or seven episodes of pitching forward, passing out, being revived, being replaced on the branch and pitching forward again, the buzzards gave up. Now, when you pulled the wire and released their feet, they sat there, saying in clear, nonverbal terms: "We tried that before. It did not work. We are not going to try it again." Now the film makers had to fly in a high-powered animal trainer to restore buzzard self-esteem. It was all a big mess; Larry McMurtry got a wonderful story out of it; and we, in turn, get the best possible parable of the workings of habit and timidity.

Why tell this crazy story here? Because Limerick uses McMurtry's story to make a point about the habit and timidity of academic writers. "Twelve buzzards hanging upside down from a tree branch," Limerick writes, "was not what Hollywood wanted from the West, but that's what

Hollywood had produced." Limerick's parable also gets us thinking about what Illich and others have identified as "the hidden curriculum." When tutors arrive in our centers, with their academic writing baggage in tow, we should be asking ourselves and them whether what schooling has produced is, in fact, what was intended. Who knew that even buzzard school produced a hidden curriculum and that even filmmakers must take care that cast members are learning what producers and directors intend to teach and not some other, even more intractable, lesson? As directors, our staff education decisions will either foster this hidden curriculum of habit and timidity or it will encourage tutors to break free of what binds them. So what's it going to be?

How often do we keep our tutors' feet (and minds and imaginations) wired by strict policies, by a reliance on a scripted approach to tutoring when we could be letting them fly free and embrace the thought every now and again of flying off in conference with writers?

If we were truly asking our tutors to work from their experiences and knowledge and questions as writers, we would never want to put them in the situation of being buzzards—as writers or as tutors. We would instead encourage them to become ever more cognizant of their writing choices and why they make the choices they do. We would ask them to let writers in on how they read assignments. We would ask them to help those writers learn to make writing choices and own them, learn the questions they can ask their teachers when they're stuck, and learn the challenges they can carry back to their professors when they want to push the boundaries of assignments.

Perhaps we're idealistic, but we believe that tutors working from what they know (and don't know) as writers may be the ones most ready to encourage other writers to take responsibility, and may be the ones most inclined to bring that third, spectral presence in the conference—the teacher—back into the equation. We can understand why some might feel the teacher is most present in the writing center, is most easily invited into the writing center, and (perhaps more importantly) is most willing to visit, when asked to describe just how an assignment should be written. But we ask in return, Is that really bringing a colleague's life as a thinker, writer, and teacher into your writing center? For example, will tutors have the opportunity in those meetings to speak back to the faculty person, to raise writing issues inherent in the assignment, or to suggest the faculty person adjust the expectations or goals or requirements of the assignment? Is this a faculty member who has managed—since finishing graduate school, getting tenure, whatever—to free herself of the wire that surely once bound her own feet? And finally, how many faculty—really, be honest—want to end up reading exactly the same assignment, and we mean exactly (because those tutors can take direction if you ask them to listen), ten or twenty or fifty times once those papers are turned in, because every student who visited the writing center listened to just what the tutor said mimicking just what the professor said? If we encourage writer and tutor to be buzzards, what's the corpse? Student writers' texts? Circling, circling, circling, waiting for the last gasp. We have greater hopes for our tutors than Hollywood had for those buzzards. They are more than (over)trained extras in the drama (or satire) of students writing for faculty.

We know the concerns: What if my tutors, working from the writing experiences they have, make mistakes in conferences? [Note to self: Tutors will make mistakes in conferences. Get used to it. Anyone who teaches—and hence makes, on average, 7.2 mistakes per class period—should understand.] What if they tell psychology students to use MLA citation because they use MLA on English papers? What if they tell writers to begin with a story because they always begin with stories, but Professor X hates stories at the beginning and could have told your staff that? What if, as in the meta-cognitive writing we saw at the beginning of this chapter, tutors assume that every writer is like them? Is that really any better than assuming every Paper #2 should be written the same way?

Every now and then, in our writing center meetings, we will realize that all the immediate issues or troubling or extraordinarily satisfying conferences in a given week have considered the same assignment being written by different writers. Or maybe two tutors raise different issues from conferences that sound as if they were working with the same assignment. Here's what the group will do, knowing they are likely never to have a conversation with the faculty person teaching the assignment in question. Everyone who held a conference that week with a student writing the assignment in question will describe the conference—What was the assignment? Did you see the assignment? What did you notice about it? Recreate the assignment for us. What did the student tell you about the assignment? What did you suggest to the student? Why did you suggest that? (Because you would always write this type of assignment in this way? Why? Because you have some idea of what you think the professor wants? Because you write this way? Because you have read widely?) There are no formulaic answers to these questions, and as tutors hear the shared responses, particularly if the responses are shared by a diverse staff, the fetters that have kept those buzzard feet firmly in place seem to loosen a little. There are many right answers; there are many ways to participate in a tutoring session. Thomas Newkirk makes this point when he thinks about James Berlin's argument that a student's "'true self' is subtly constructed by the responses of others in the class'" (Berlin qtd. in Newkirk 6). We keep asking ourselves—as Newkirk did—when we work with writers, "What kind of 'self' are we inviting students to become? What kinds of 'selves' do we subtly dismiss?"

Like the perspectives essays, these meeting conversations broaden tutors' conceptions of their own writing and tutoring choices and require tutors to consider what they invite and what they dismiss when they use their own writing experiences as the lens for work with writers in conferences. In comparing approaches as writers and tutors, we are brought back to the many possible directions of conferences or writing. And the staff has the opportunity to revise their understanding of conferences they've had, students they've met with, and assignments they've seen. When there is room for every writer on staff to share individual beliefs about writing and the writing process, to question those beliefs, and to re-examine them, there is room for more than one approach to any assignment. As a result, there are fewer motionless, thoughtless buzzards perched about the writing center. Our tutors' self-examination of their experiences as writers and tutors should embody the same reflective practices we seek to prioritize in writing center conferences. If we strive for reflective practice from our tutors in conference, we should stress in our work with our staff that "we learn to understand ourselves through explaining ourselves to others. To do this, we rely on a reflection that involves a *checking* against, a *confirming*, and a *balancing* of self with others" (Yancey 11).

TOWARD A COMMUNITY OF PRACTICE

It is this reflection about self in relation to others that is the focus of the final part of this chapter. Fostering writerly identity is not our ultimate goal; it is how those identities participate in a writing center community of practice that is most important. We turn again to Wenger to help us explain. He tells us that participants in a community of practice must be engaged in activities that are meaningful and must have ways of talking about those experiences, that there must be a way of "talking about . . . shared historical and social resources . . . that can sustain mutual engagement in action," that participants' competence must be recognized, and that there must be "a way of talking about how learning changes who we are and creates personal histories of becoming in the context of our communities" (4–5). That's a tall order, but it's also an invitation to playful, creative work, work that is organic, work that grows from our writing center staffs, not work that is imposed upon them by a one-size-fits-all template.

Facilitating writerly identities and full participation in the writing center community requires adaptability on everyone's part. Such facilitation draws on individual strengths and mitigates individual weaknesses. Projects should work to make the familiar strange and the strange familiar. Take one fairly common writing center project as an example: the production of a writing center newsletter. Producing such a newsletter is a frequently cited PR strategy for writing centers, and working on a newsletter may appeal to tutors with journalistic aspirations or tutors who like to play around with design and layout. Newsletters can also, however, seem contrived and formulaic, decidedly curricular. Samples abound, a mouse-click away, all with discouragingly familiar features—a tutor's corner, grammar tips, sample websites. It is too easy to lift a template and engage in the sort of mindless repetition and routinization our epigraph to this chapter warns against. Instead, tutors might reflect on what else a newsletter can be. They might bring together the purpose of the activity with the goals of the staff, goals that certainly include modeling with and for each other the development and sustenance of a learning community. Create a truly collaborative newsletter, one that showcases the range of writerly participation and language play in the writing center. Disrupt the traditional newsletter format. They might bring your creative writers and your journalists together and have them compose a newsletter in verse. Your budding CIA agent or resident tutorial linguist might be interested in encrypting one. No more Halloween candy drawings. How about a prize instead for the first student to crack the code?

We and our tutors have tried filmmaking, which requires (among other things) screenwriting and editing talents and draws tutors into performative realms.[3] If these projects are to be meaningful, though, they need to grow out of tutor interests and talents, and they need to be problem-posing activities that support a collective sense of purpose among our tutors. We're thinking here not of mock tutorials that purport to address tutoring issues/problems in an end-game sort of way. Rather, these films portray scenarios, often humorously, that the tutors have experienced as problematic. They are teaching tools designed by the tutors so that they, and sometimes a conference audience (as was the case when the Plymouth State tutors showed their films at IWCA 2005), may think together about the meaning of these issues and even about the ways the scenarios are portrayed. Does the humor border on stereotyping? Are there a variety of ways to handle a difficult situation? The key to any of these activities is, of course, that they cannot be dropped whole into just any writing center, nor can they be predictably used from year to year as some people use their yellowed course notes. Tutors must be actively engaged in designing and implementing such projects if those projects are to remain meaningful.

In addition to encouraging new, fresh activities, we also recognize the value of ritual and tradition in our writing centers, not the kind of ritual that Spellmeyer calls "routinization," but the kind that brings tutors to a "time out of time."[4] Nowhere is this more evident than in the long-running tutor journals housed in one of our centers. Journals, as you may have noticed in your own center, can be decidedly curricular, surprisingly anti-curricular, and everything in between. In our experience, early entries resemble buzzard-feet writing. Tutors are writing to an imagined academic audience—the teacher (or in this case, the director). Tutors dutifully write about their heroism in saving the poor writer, or wire their own feet into the role of "bad" tutor—"I talked too much during the session," "I gave the writer too much information." The entries are boring, uninspired, cardboard, junk food. Later entries (and, in some cases, we mean years later) are increasingly integrated into the fabric of everyday life in the center, providing frequent opportunities for genuine moments of discovery and inviting the type of checking, confirming and balancing Yancey says is at the center of writers' reflections.

These journals are not the usual sort of writing encouraged by the major tutor manuals—they aren't regulatory in the sense that the entries are written to a director who uses them to check up on the tutors, nor are they written as reports to faculty. Tutors write for each other. About whatever they want. They are paid to write for one hour every week—they're actually *paid* to write. They think that's cool. They also know that the writing is done on epochal time—in other words, a tutor might skip the scheduled journal hour and write later on during the week–at home, during breakfast, at one in the morning. Sometimes there are a couple of weeks that go by, and then one person will write two or three entries in the binder that holds a year's worth of writing—the binder that stays in the tutor lounge. The binder that everyone reaches for at the beginning of each shift.

As the tutors become increasingly responsible for constructing rather than simply receiving knowledge, as they construct meaning and share competence, and talk about learning, both in and out of the classroom, the journals illustrate the complexity of an organic system, one that incorporates and often celebrates the tutors' life experiences, their conflicts, their failures, their successes. Here, there is evidence of an ongoing, non-linear, many times irreverent/trickster-like inquiry into complex and challenging ideas and an enactment of the kind of collaboration that is truly generative. These journals can sometimes be written for the individual alone, sometimes in response to other entries, but they always keep other tutors in mind, rather than the director. *They* are each other's readers, and they develop a finely-honed sense of audience and purpose, one that gives them a way, as Wenger says, "of talking about . . . shared historical and social resources." As one tutor wrote, "I was thinking on the way over here about this journal book and how it will probably be the most permanent and most read of all the writing that I have done in five years."

Journals that serve to regulate tutor knowledge and experience can be remarkably linear and sterile, but the journal that moves beyond such regulation can invent and reinvent itself, allowing for risk, for failure, for ebullience. Although the journals sometimes tend toward (to use the language of chaos theory) entropy or dissipation at times (there can be periods of slapstick silliness, for example), there is an overall evolution of philosophy, of purpose, of theory, of practice—precisely because tutors receive and reflect upon feedback from their peers. When they flip through the older journals, they benefit from the insights of tutors long gone (that shared historical perspective again) and frequently, the current tutors bring the voices and thoughts of the previous staff into their current conversations and ruminations.

Amy, for example, writes her first journal entry on September 1, 1998, concerned about how she'll fit into the tutor culture. She feels better when, during her first hour, she looks through the "old journal logs" and sees "quite a few entries were from the experienced tutors giving advice to the newcomers." However, she notes, "It seemed hard for them to remember back to when they started and couldn't quite hit upon what they needed to hear when they first started here." Amy makes a list of the questions *she* has in that moment so that when it's her turn to give advice, she'll be able to look back at this journal, back to this present, and remember. In doing so, she explicitly attempts to avoid reinscribing the master-novice model that she might otherwise soon be able to enact. As Wenger tells us, "As trajectories, our identities incorporate the past and the future in the very process of negotiating the present" (155). Amy also highlights the sense of audience and purpose to which we alluded earlier and recognizes, in those very first days on the job, that the writing center affords a very different sense of institutional rhythm and memory, one that she is unlikely to encounter elsewhere on campus, one that offers a future view of herself in the writing center. This future relies on her participation in the community of practice, and she thinks (unknowingly enacting Weick's sense of the future perfect), "Someone will have wanted my answers." So she writes with specificity and with an eye toward what will be needed in the future. Here's Wenger again: Our identities, he says, are changed by learning, and we come to the ability to understand ourselves as a combination of the past present and future in the present. "We are always simultaneously dealing with specific situations, participating in the histories of certain practices, and involved in becoming certain persons" (155). We feel ever more convinced that it is important for our tutors to have the opportunity to write their way to becoming certain persons and to chronicle that journey, not just for themselves but for others.

As tutors write the interconnections of their lives outside and inside the writing center, consider and critique the writing they and their peers are asked to do in classes, and produce texts from within the center itself, they are not simply writers reenacting the roles others have scripted. Instead, the journals themselves serve a ritualistic function, deliberately attending to the symbolic realm of negotiated literacy practices, resulting in the creation of artifacts that do not stand alone but are inscribed in the process of re-enacting, re-negotiating, and experiencing self and community. This more deliberative attention to tutors' identities as writers supports the de-schooling and de-routinizing of their writing practices (and perhaps ours, as well). In true dialogue with one another, writers in any writing center discover the meanings that attend to and emerge from the practice of writing. With careful guidance and attention, these practices can turn writers toward attunement with the world, to the ways in which their being in the world informs their pedagogical work and, correspondingly, to the ways in which their pedagogical work informs their being in the world.

6

EVERYDAY RACISM
Anti-Racism Work and Writing Center Practice

Not everything that is faced can be changed, but nothing can be changed until it is faced.

James A. Baldwin

As we have drafted the chapters of this book, we have had the benefit of being in conversation not only with each other but also with the network of tutors and directors brought together and sustained by organizations like the International Writing Centers Association (IWCA), National Conference on Peer Tutoring in Writing (NCPTW), Summer Institute, and various regional writing center associations. Through those interactions, we have discovered that neither being a long time activist nor a well-intentioned and principled individual inoculates any of us or the spaces in which we work against racism. Everyone has a story, many stories, to tell. And yet, conversations about race and racism in our culture are among the most puzzling and provocative discussions in which to engage. This work can neither be done perfectly nor completely; it is an ongoing process.

The racism in our writing centers, like racism across our institutions, communities, and across the social, political, and economic landscape of our lives, is not a series of aberrations, but the everyday manifestation of deeply embedded logics and patterns. When we make the choice to notice, mourn, and struggle against racism in our individual and professional lives, we are not alone. And when we realize in our own centers that, despite our careful attention to race and racism, despite our tutors' and our own best intentions, more work needs to be done, we are not alone then either.

We lost Krista, an African American student at a predominantly white private college who enrolled in and thrived in her *Peer Tutoring in Writing* course. She became fascinated with the field and began to talk with her teacher (the director of the college's writing center) about the possibility of a writing center career and about her desire to work as a tutor. When Krista did begin working in the center, however, the white tutors repeatedly failed to recognize her when she came to work. Each time she entered the writing center, she was asked by her colleagues if she needed to schedule an appointment. Krista, who is also a single mother, ended her employment after another tutor, upon meeting Krista's son for the first time, exclaimed, "Jared will be an awesome basketball player someday!"

This story is interesting—and troubling—because of what it suggests about how dominant images of people of color in the white imagination are operative inside the writing center and that these images can impact how tutors recognize, receive, and respect (or not) one another. The tutors in this story were unable to conceive of an African American woman who possessed the knowledge, abilities, and skills to be a tutor. She must, they thought, need help. These tutors were well-intentioned: they wanted to help. They didn't consciously set out to dishonor Krista. The highly racialized lenses through which they were able to see her, however, distorted their vision. Even their attempts to recognize her strengths, and those of her son, were distorted by prevailing images of African American women and men distributed wholesale throughout dominant American culture. As principled and well-intentioned as the white tutors were, they interacted with Krista and with her son through the haze of a deeply internalized sense of white superiority.

Of course, tutors of color working in our writing centers need to worry not only about how their fellow tutors will perceive them; they also must worry, even more perhaps, about how they will be received by the writers they work with. Another example: An African American graduate student tutor sits down with a Russian undergraduate working on a paper for an upper-level writing requirement. The student has inflected a current events paper with what the tutor perceives as racist rhetoric. When the tutor pushes the student to think about her argument, the student pushes back: she thought her tutor was going to be one of the white tutors and wondered aloud about her tutor's qualifications. In response, the tutor offers both her qualifications and her life history.

Though this story shares with the previous one some implicit sense of what a "real" tutor looks like, it raises a number of additional questions we might consider: In what ways does the student's sense of her own whiteness intersect with her immigrant status to produce an expectation and desire for a white American tutor as the norm? What factors have eased and/or troubled this student's own assimilation into racial rules and order, both in America and in her country of origin?

The tutor's response is also troubling. She explains after the incident that she "chalked it up to a combination of immigrant inexperience and a lack of cultural knowledge." She tells us she rehearsed her credentials for the writer in order to reassure her. If systemic racism works to convince whites that they are inherently better and therefore deserve the privileges that accrue to them through racism, it also works to convince people of color that they are not quite good enough—or at least that they must continually demonstrate that they are good enough, because their qualifications are always in doubt. People of color internalize their own oppression much as whites internalize superiority. These perceptions become the part of the lens through which we see the everyday—and they make everyday racism seem normal, natural, only to be expected.

Racism certainly has not always seemed normal to us. As children, we may have deemed someone's race worthy of notice, but we didn't always deem it worthy of judgment. That racist lesson is one we learned through everyday interactions, and it is one we must actively work to unlearn. As activist Beth Roy asserts:

> Racism teaches white children to be silent. We notice racial differences ("Why does Peter have such curly hair?") and we are told it is impolite to comment ("Hush! You'll hurt his feelings"). We question injustices ("Why don't we let Mary, our housekeeper, eat dinner with us?") and we are told not to ask ("That's just the way it is.") or that our perception is wrong ("She doesn't want to eat with us."). We seek connection ("Can't I go play basketball in the park?") and we are told people of color are dangerous ("No. That's not a good neighborhood.").
>
> Eventually we stop asking, commenting, questioning. If we can't speak about race and we stop seeing social injustices, eventually we lose awareness of injustice in general—those done *to* us and well as those done *by* us. (Roy 15)

Perhaps we need not stop asking, commenting and questioning. In *Communities of Practice*, Etienne Wenger writes, "Through engagement in practice, we see first-hand the effects we have on the world and discover how the world treats the likes of us. We explore our ability to engage with one another, how we can participate in activities, what we can and cannot do" (192). And as our epigraph reveals, "nothing can be changed until it is faced." So how do we want our tutors, how do *we* want to engage with issues of racial identity as they present themselves in the writing center? We should all be asking, by this point in the book, what kinds of learning our current system of staff development offers, what kinds of learning we want to promote, and what moves we want to make with our tutors and the writers who use our centers.

Much of Wenger's understanding of a community of practice involves exploring the relationship between identity and social organization. Critical race theorists also recognize the power of that relationship and have argued convincingly that nothing shapes identity in more compelling ways than racial identity does. It is for this reason that, although we have talked about diversity throughout this book, we choose to foreground this discussion of race. When we imagine our writing centers as learning cultures, we enact a hopeful, participatory model for education, one that is poised to engage in transformative institutional work. As we change our own understandings of ourselves in relation to others, we become change-agents in our other, overlapping communities of practice. Wenger writes, "[L]earning—whatever form it takes—changes who we are by changing our ability to participate, to belong, to negotiate meaning" (226).

In the course of writing this book, we have spent hundreds of hours in conversation. We have asked ourselves what kinds of learning have shaped us and how those influences affect our lives and practice. Because we are five white women, we are aware that there are experiences or observations that directors of color would be able to bring to this discussion that we simply cannot.[1] We begin from where we are, listening to, facing and questioning the legacies each of us brings to this work. Even though we share many similarities in our thinking about race, we come to our very similar positions through very different histories, histories that include interracial families, hired household "help," and human rights activism. We have learned again that there is no way to talk about race without also talking about hopes, fears, pain, and pride. We are well aware of the variety of ways in which the work is painful. We also know the ways in which the work is profoundly satisfying, brings joy and a sense of authenticity, enables new and deeper friendships and loving relationships with family members of color, challenges us to think more and better, to do more meaningful work in our writing centers, and to live our principles more fully. We do not mean to suggest that beginning or carrying on a study of, conversation about, or struggle against racism is easy or risk-free. We do mean to suggest that it is necessary to begin even though beginning may seem difficult and risky.

WHY COMMIT TO THE WORK?

As we think about the silence that we work against in this chapter and in our writing centers, we realize that it is this silence that enables racism to flourish, to a large extent, because structural inequalities are perceived as so normal, so natural, that they are invisible to most white people. All evidence (from our own and other centers, from recent scholarship) suggests that writing centers are sites where staff members recognize and, in many cases experience, racism. Imagining that we get to choose whether or not to make this work part of our mission is one more manifestation of the privilege we enjoy as white directors.[2] Consequently, we believe that we must consciously and consistently recognize that racism is an everyday experience for students, tutors, and directors of color, and concomitantly, that the benefits and advantages that accrue to white people as a result of racism are an everyday experience for white students, tutors, and directors—like the five of us. We suggest that writing centers need to be involved in anti-racism work on their own campuses and beyond, even though the work is hard, especially when it may challenge our cherished views of ourselves as fair and impartial and our centers as inherently inclusive. Racism is not something we implicitly endorse, we tell ourselves, in our hiring practices, nor something we can explicitly address in our staff education. Establishing a canon that leads to the development of "textbook" IWCA writing centers (as we have heard people describe their sites) is not at odds with the goal of transforming our institutions. Or is it?

Because this kind of reflection is hard and continuous, we would not be surprised to hear, "I'm so busy talking with faculty, working on curriculum, training tutors, and negotiating with administrators. I don't have time to be an anti-racist too." Here's a hard truth: Laments about a lack of time are never simply about a lack of time. They are statements about priorities. They are expressions of fear. They mask concerns about exposing inadequacies. We understand. Adding antiracism work to our writing center agenda might seem like a burden, a foolish choice, something only a glutton for punishment would take on. Because we are rarely encouraged by our institutional leaders to incorporate this work into our everyday, we avoid it, resist it. We can say it is about our time (I have enough to do already), our kind of institution (we don't need this; or we need it badly, but I doubt anything would change), our personal and professional priorities (my work is in feminist theory), our defensiveness (I know I am not a racist), or our discomfort (I don't know how to deal with this).

A common objection to studying and working against racism specifically is that there are other forms of oppression, such as sexism, classism, and homophobia for which critical race theory and anti-racism do not account. While we acknowledge the importance of working for justice in these other crucial areas, we offer anti-racism work as a place to begin for what we believe to be compelling reasons: Racism cuts through multiple identities and magnifies the effects and impact of other manifestations of oppression. The experience of people of color who are also women, working class, and/or gay is markedly different from the experiences of whites who share those other identities. To study and talk deliberately and intentionally about racism suggests neither a denial of the suffering of whites under other forms of oppression nor does it preclude studying the ways in which multiple identities and forms of oppression overlap or intersect. To attempt that study, however, without accounting for racism is to reproduce it. Further, we argue, it behooves those of us who are committed to social justice to consider carefully the ways in which racism has often been used to prevent the formation of meaningful coalitions among oppressed groups (the differences between African-American and white feminists is a case in point). In fact, racism is *the* place to start, because until we are willing and equipped to address it, we will be unable to resist other forms of oppression that intersect with and are informed by it.

We realize that since writing centers are situated within institutions which are themselves implicated in the power structures that wittingly or unwittingly foster racism, they cannot completely escape resembling and reproducing much of what students of color experience outside of our spaces. But writing centers are also spaces where people deliberately seek "opportunities for greater insight" (Tatum 201) into themselves and others. If we have communities of practice that are diverse in the places where meaning is negotiated, where fields of experience are shared, where people write, learn, and talk together, then we have, at least potentially, a set of conditions in which anti-racism work might productively begin.

And when each of us has begun, taking even the most tentative steps toward reading to understand race and racism, by opening conversations with tutors and student writers, with colleagues, we may feel uneasy. What if, we worry, people get mad at us, get mad at each other, what if the community of our writing center comes completely undone? We take heart, however, from Wenger's compelling argument that dissent and contestation, far from being antithetical to authentic community, are necessary to it. He writes, "[A] community of practice is neither a haven of togetherness nor an island of intimacy insulated from political and social relations. Disagreement, challenges, and competition can all be forms of participation. In fact, as a form of participation, rebellion often reveals a greater commitment than does passive conformity" (77).

We have asked ourselves, "What if I make a mistake? What if I say or do the wrong thing?" And these questions sound familiar because they are the same concerns our tutors express to us about tutoring. To them we say: "Yes, you *might* make a mistake." We say, "You're learning." We say, "You know more than you think you know." We say, "You don't have to have all the answers." And we have to give ourselves the same permission. We have to give our tutors the opportunity to learn with us and to teach us about race and racism.

We submit that, although we will make mistakes, we can and must learn to see racism and respond responsibly to it. In the remaining sections of this chapter, we offer a brief overview of the ways that racism is defined and categorized and suggest possibilities for restructuring staff education and writing center energy to engage more effectively in antiracist efforts in our own "sphere[s] of influence" (Tatum 204). And in the appendix to this chapter (p.107), we provide further practical materials, including a reading list.

UNDERSTANDING RACISM

When we think of racism, we tend to think first of overt forms such as the crossburnings of the Ku Klux Klan, of the black and white photographs of "colored" water fountains, or the explicitly racist lyrics of white supremacist rock bands. Critical race theories, however, suggest that racism is a more complex phenomenon than can be accounted for by definitions that focus on individual thoughts, predispositions, and actions. An alternative and more productive definition must account for the adaptability of racism to assert itself in particular historical moments and social contexts. The manifestations of racism have changed over time, moving from legalized and highly explicit forms (slavery, miscegenation, Jim Crow laws, etc.) to current masked or coded racism deeply entrenched in institutional logics, structures, and systems. As we've thought about and talked about and written about racism, it has helped us to have language that identifies its varying forms. Relying on that language and the ways that different, very complex types of racism may be defined has, for example, made us more aware of the differences between institutional racism and racial prejudice, the latter seemingly more obvious and personal, the former more insidious, far-reaching, and therefore more difficult to address, especially from within.

We've seen such institutional racism in all its forms at work in our own home institutions, for example, in a university recently marked as the fifth most homogenous university in the nation by the *Princeton Review*. In its coverage of this story, the campus newspaper notes that minority enrollments have actually decreased by nearly 50% in the past three years.[3] The rest of the article highlights the university's commitment to increasing diversity on campus and the recent "hiring of eight diverse professors," leaving out the question of why minority enrollments would be dropping so precipitously. In speaking with a tutor who is also an editor of the newspaper, we asked whether anyone had looked into the fact that the university only reached its all-time high of 14% minority enrollment by instituting a short-lived football team, a sport which was phased out three years ago. "Hmmm. . ." she said, raising her eyebrows. Clearly, we couldn't have been the only ones on our campus to notice this troubling fact. But more often than not, instances of racism like this one receive only a "Hmmm . . .," and a pause, most often by white students, faculty and staff who are unsure of what else they might do or say.

We five have worked to break that silence in our writing centers and in our institutions, and we've found that the first conversations need to start with a kind of naming and framing for ourselves and those we work with. Sometimes, anti-racism work involves naming assumptions, behaviors, policies, and institutional practices as racist. But this naming does not always involve direct confrontation or purposeful conflagration. Just as when we tutor or teach, we need to have an array of strategies from which to draw. And just as when we tutor or teach, any of the range of strategies we might employ are meaningless unless they are framed by a grasp of the theories, philosophies, and scholarship that informed their development. We need to learn how to read and analyze what we see before us (the racially informed experiences of our everyday life and work) in order to make informed and productive decisions about what we will do. We need to know the *whys* of race and racism in order to discern the *hows* of anti-racism.

Anti-racist activists share a commonly held definition of racism supported by current critical theories of race, racial formation, and racism. The definition comes in several variations, but all of them contain the same essential ingredients: Racism is race prejudice magnified, enforced, and reproduced by systemic and institutional power.[4] Racism, according to this definition, is characterized most particularly by the abuse of power within the institutions and systems that shape all of our lives–including the high schools, colleges, and universities in which we learn, teach, and tutor. In order to be able to use this definition to teach and tutor against racism, though, we also need to understand power and its operations. According to the Crossroads and the Tri-Council Coordinating Commission/Minnesota Collaborative Anti-Racism Initiative (both anti-racist training, organizing, and activist groups) power is defined "as if it were cubed" (3). Here's what they say:

1. Power, at its first level, operates over people of color by oppressing, marginalizing, denying access and opportunity, and dehumanizing them. (This level is often where even the most well-meaning among us stop in our analysis of racism).
2. Power, at its second level, ensures that whites will receive benefits and advantages denied to people of color and that those privileges will be invisible or seem natural and normal to us.
3. Power, at its third level, operates by socializing both whites and people of color into acceptance of and obedience to "racial rules."

In sum, these theorists and activists understand that we are socialized into (not born with) particular raced identities which are then used to determine, categorize, evaluate, sort, promote, or reject us. This socialization, then, is the work of the vast array of systems and institutions through which our social, political, intellectual, and spiritual lives are conditioned.

For many of us, to think about racism in these ways is to be profoundly unsettled, yet it may be accepting that unsettled feeling that will help us identify and name the racism that surrounds us in our everyday. So much, we believe, of what draws folks to writing center work is our individual and collective investment in being careful, caring, and reflective in teaching and talking with students about their writing. To begin to realize and account for the possibility that racism is woven into that identity too, wound through even those practices that we hope are expressions of our most dearly-held principles, is to experience profound dislocation. The understanding of racism offered above does not invalidate that which is at the heart of our work in writing centers—the principles and commitments to responsive practice. On the contrary, when we try to engage with this understanding of racism, rather than ignoring or dismissing it, our work is enhanced. This engagement also implies the hard recognition that all of us are implicated, to one degree or another, in such a power structure. However, this recognition is essential if we are to think creatively and at multiple levels about how we work with students and tutors, how we teach tutors to work with writers and one another, and how we work within our institutions and our profession. Remember the notions of leadership we introduced in our first chapter? Structural leaders have a leadership role because of their positions within institutions, but functional leaders assume leadership roles out of a sense of mission, need, and purpose and require the participation of others to accomplish this purpose (Tagg 338). We are not the only ones who need to learn and revisit definitions of racism, but if we take on functional leadership roles, we, in writing centers, may be uniquely poised to "use the authority of [our] offices to achieve the mission of institutional transformation" (Tagg 339).

"TUTOR TRAINING" AND RACE

Our profession has done little to date to complicate tutors' or our own understandings of racism in relation to our individual and professional identities, our teaching and tutoring work, or our institutions. Just as the label "tutor training" seems an outdated term for describing our work with tutors, so too do our available "tutor training" texts seem outdated in their abilities to suggest ways of incorporating meaningful considerations of race in our staff education practices.[5]

An examination of tutor education textbooks suggests a very particular and limited understanding of race in writing centers. Older texts, including standards like Muriel Harris's *Teaching One-to-One: The Writing Conference* and *The High School Writing Center: Establishing and Maintaining One,* edited by Pamela B. Farrell, neglect to mention race or racism. Given their initial publication dates, we do not find this omission surprising, and it would not be quite so troubling except for the fact that these texts (especially Harris's) continue to be influential in the field. The texts that follow them do little or nothing to redress the problem. Some recent ones follow the model set by yet another classic, Meyer and Smith's *The Practical Tutor,* which includes a chapter addressing general matters of diversity. Unfortunately, such chapters tend to be framed in deficit terms. For example, McAndrew and Reigstad's book, *Tutoring Writing: A Practical Guide for Conferences,* includes a chapter entitled "Tutoring *Different* People" (our emphasis). This chapter begins by addressing alternative grammars, then moves in sequence to "gender differences," "multicultural and ESL writers and tutors," "learning disabled writers," and thence to "personalities and learning styles." While McAndrew and Reigstad make some compelling moves in the chapter, including advocating the hiring of "multicultural tutors," the framing of the chapter and the bulk of its content suggest a very particular notion of who is "different" and, by extension, who is "normal" or "like *us*." Rafoth's edited collection *A Tutor's Guide: Helping Writers One to One* likewise situates the discussion of racism within a single chapter, "Teaching in Emotionally Charged Situations," and specifically addresses only the use of racial slurs within a discussion of offensive language.

When the white writers and editors of the textbooks mentioned above limit their exploration of racism to addressing simply language, they reflect a *commonsense* understanding of what racism is (simply a matter of individual prejudice) and how it operates. The framing or containing of racism within these texts is not unique to writing centers, but rather reflects misconceptions and under-education about race and racism that are broadly shared across all strata of American society as well as American higher education writ large. By asking for anti-racism work to appear in the everyday of a writing center, we seek to crack apart the artificial containment of racism within carefully managed, constrained, and negatively constructed narrative structures (chapters, paragraphs, sound bytes, hearsay, memes). Rather than clinging to narrow and under-theorized definitions and approaches, we advocate more sustained examinations of the ways and degrees to which writing centers might be contact zones in which there is an ongoing struggle to challenge the unequal distribution of power and access along racial lines.

All of us want to honor the multivocality inherent in writing center work. As students will be in dialogue with students in our writing center, why not have texts in dialogue with texts? We suggest, therefore, including readings by scholars of color (writers like bell hooks, Beverly Tatum, Elaine Richardson, Richard Rodriguez, Victor Villanueva, and Min-Zhan Lu, to name a few) to enhance and complicate the work of white scholars (Muriel Harris, Stephen North, and Kenneth Bruffee, for example). We also suggest readings that might enable directors and tutors to talk about whiteness and white privilege. (Paula Rothenberg's "White Privilege: Essential Readings from the Other Side of Racism" comes to mind here.) All of us have, for example, used the following inventory (adapted from Peggy McIntosh's "Unpacking the Invisible Backpack"[6]) of white privilege, revised for tutors in predominantly white institutions.

1. I can feel secure in the knowledge that my success or failure in any class I take will not be attributed to my race.

2. I can feel secure in the knowledge that I will not be asked by any professor to speak for my race.

3. I can feel assured that no one will assume that I was only admitted to this institution because of affirmative action.

4. I can feel assured that my classmates and professors will believe that I earned admission to this institution.

5. I can feel assured that in almost every class I take I will be introduced to and given the opportunity to study the history, literature, and discoveries of people who look like me.

6. I can feel assured that most people will not assume I am at this institution on an athletic scholarship.

7. I can feel assured that most people will not assume I am a science or math major based on my race.

8. I can feel assured that professors will not doubt the authorship of my writing on the basis of my race.

9. My home language and the language in which I am expected to speak and write for class are comfortably similar.

10. I can feel assured that when a professor identifies "errors" in my papers, he or she will not attribute them to my race or to my "dialect."

11. When I am tutoring or mentoring or assisting a professor, I can be assured that other students and faculty will recognize and respect my qualifications and credentials.

12. I don't have to worry about whether or not people like me based on my race.

13. I don't have to worry about whether or not or when to try "passing" for someone of another race.

14. When I see images in mainstream popular culture that are meant to suggest beauty, I see images of people of my race.

15. I can feel assured that my friends and acquaintances won't make assumptions about how I am in bed based on my race.

16. If someone says something I think is racist in my presence, I may choose whether or not to respond. I do not feel an obligation to intervene on behalf of myself or my family or home community.

17. I can be assured that most of my professors, fellow students, and the staff and administrators of my institution will be people of my race.

18. I can be assured that if I need to speak to an authority figure at my school, that person will be of my race.

19. I can be late to class or to my job (or tutorial) at the writing center without fear that my lateness will be attributed to my race.

20. If I have a negative encounter in class or out of class, with students, faculty, or staff, I don't need to wonder or worry whether what happened had racial overtones.

After filling out the inventory, tutors write a reflection. Writing shared by one staff of graduate student tutors sounds like this:

> Nearly four years ago, I found myself at a different graduate institution thinking about these questions of race, achievement and societal stereotypes, wondering and hoping about whether my experience would change as I advanced professionally and as discussions of privilege became more visible. Unfortunately, I have discovered that the structures that support social injustice have only become more visible in the position I am in now as a graduate student in a doctoral program.
>
> *
>
> These questions reinforce how difficult it is for me to address race and racism. [In] a course I am in this semester, one student said in class that despite three other white students and myself are "nice and open people," she would never share experiences with us because we are white. She is someone I consider a friend and respect as a peer in my department. Her remark jolted me immensely.
>
> *
>
> As a women's studies PhD student, I find myself responding to this "list" in somewhat surprising ways. Surprising, most especially . . . the cruel realities of the different types of oppressive systems at work in this list feel more raw than ever. As a White, educated, middle-class student, the responsibility I feel as an educator and writing center tutor seems more intense.

We don't claim that using this inventory will magically transform the writing center, but we do believe that it might be a valuable tool to use to begin confronting white privilege. Other considerations for staff education might be fiction or non-fiction that represents the mix of cultures on your campus, or selections from student authors, tutors and others, writing back to racism and/or to readings about racism. Here's an example of what can happen when a diverse staff of tutors bring their own rich backgrounds into dialogue with the work of diverse scholars who are, because of the structure of the course, in dialogue with one another. These are also examples of the kind of writing we talked about earlier, writing that engages identity formation, writing that combines past, present and future selves.

Kathryn writes about her final paper for the tutoring class:

> I took a risk [during our workshop] by explaining my racist family to the tutors, hoping that they would understand and not judge me because of my parents' beliefs. I am not racist; as I said in my paper, "Luckily, I was smart enough to figure out that my parents did not have all the answers." In this paper, I wanted to explain where I came from, but also where I was going. . . .
>
> Although writing about this topic challenged me, I know that it was hardly a struggle by comparison. We had read about [the struggles] of other people: Gloria Anzaldua . . . bell hooks [. . . and] Min-Zhan Lu . . . They made my difficulties seem insignificant, because I'd never experienced anything as difficult as these people. I had a new respect for people who have dealt with such struggles, and I felt ready to work with people who may have had serious problems in their lives.

At this point, Kathryn has engaged with the readings, but has had very little exposure to her own racial construction. We see her tentatively reaching toward a future self, one less constrained by her past, one that is on a more hopeful trajectory. She has taken first steps toward unlearning what she's been taught. A few months later, Kathryn hears this from Susan, a tutor from Ghana, who reads the following response to bell hooks' "When I Was a Young Soldier for the Revolution":

> "In all my writing classes, I was the only black student." These words by bell hooks practically jumped off the page and back-handed me across the face. I've heard black kids say they are the only black students in their class but only to each other, never out loud, never written down for the whole world to see. I always noticed if I was the only black, but I was never sure if others did also. I never brought it up because of the fear of being labeled "the militant black girl." I don't want to be perceived as having a chip on my shoulder.

Both of these writers engage one another from their respective subject positions. Susan sees herself as "other" in her daily (college) life, while Kathryn acknowledges what has been her privilege of only seeing self in her consideration of race. Here's another rich complication. Like Amy, both of these tutors had the opportunity to look back at what others had written over the past fifteen years, and discovered this entry from a 2002 workshop. The student, Alan, had a difficult time writing his paper. He was interested in bell hooks' discussion of her voices in "When I was a Young Soldier," in Min-Zhan Lu's essay "From Silence to Words," and in Helen Fox's *Listening to the World,* particularly in the chapters that emphasize the strong connection between culture and rhetoric. Alan is keenly aware of the politics of language, and his past writing becomes a teaching moment for the current tutors as he writes about his own conflicting writerly identities.

> For most of any given day I find that my voice is inauthentic, unsure and wavering in its speech. Simple thoughts are difficult for me to explain, basic communication is tedious and what's more than all this, I feel unreal, ephemeral as if I do not speak at all.
>
> *
>
> I shall classify this quivering speech mentioned above as, *Affected,* because indeed it is so. The reasons for this are that when I communicate in this way, it is always to white people. Now in my mind I have three options, *Ebonics, Affected,* or speak the way I write, *Arrogantly.* I usually choose affected because it sounds more like the way white folk communicate, at least to me. Yet not all white people, just some, it's casual, has very little pretense, so I try to imitate it to better communicate with my fellow man and fail miserably. It has gotten to the point where I notice it, loathe it, and try to rid my mouth and tongue of it. I seem to be losing, however, for it looks as if this way of speaking has embedded itself into my muscle memory.
>
> *
>
> The next manner of speaking is Ebonics, which is the way blacks and others in ghettos throughout the states communicate. We holla at each otha wit a kinda speech that is relaxed, laced wit mad muthafuckin' swears, but is direct and to the point. There ain't much room for fuckin' around, either make your point or get fucked up for bullshittin' a nigga. This is where I can just let my muthafuckin' balls and chill the fuck out. I feel that this is my true voice, I feel that it makes me, me. It's like I just say, fuck all you muthafuckas, this is my tongue. Ride wit it, or get rode on.
>
> *
>
> The third and final is Arrogant, flashing my mind at every turn. Sliding phrases and metaphors from great black thinkers into banal conversation, just to show I'm not like you, nor do I care to be. I find that this is what I revert to when angered by a member of the race in charge, I belittle them, insult their culture, and rue the day that Europeans came and stole us from our homes, raped our wives, and made creatures like myself, almost a member of neither race, something you can't rightly place.
>
> *
>
> Mind you this is only what happens when I try to talk to white, non-ghetto people. My voice is not one or the other all the time, it is not

homogeneous it is heterogeneous. It is a mixed bag of cultures all vying for the forefront. My mouth is often muddled because I've adopted not just the speech, but the culture behind it, and when that happens, you become a partial member of said culture, and those new words that come with it are now a part of you. Yet it is not as easy as saying choose one and stick with it. I feel like I sell out my people every time I opt out of an Ebonics word for something else. I feel like the world finds me ignorant anytime I use Ebonics in place of standard, middle class white English. And I also know that most if not all of you cannot speak Crioulo, so fuck that.

Alan is responding to the course readings, but are those readings about the violence done to students when their languages/cultures are in conflict as powerful for the tutors (for us?) as hearing this kind of writing from a peer? What kinds of risks does Alan take in writing? What kinds of risks do white tutors take in responding to that writing? But what kinds of risks do we take if we *don't* write about race, if we *don't* respond to everyday lived experience, if we don't share and listen and process our everyday experiences of race?

So how do we work toward helping us and our tutors accomplish this work? We return again to the learning culture inventory in chapter four to help us think about that. As we plan to explore "values, assumptions, belief, and expectations," we might include tutors when we decide what readings and activities will be included in our syllabi. We might ask the writers who use our centers to attend staff education meetings to speak back to the ways they are characterized in their classes and coursework. We might keep stories of our individual processes and take time for reflection by creating opportunities for us, as managers, and our tutors to write about, to reify, in Wenger's sense of the term (to participate in a community of practice by writing an account of the community), our growing communal understanding of race, racism, and whiteness. We might challenge our assumptions about hiring. As we mentioned in chapter four, instead of looking in typical places for tutors, we might actively recruit students who reflect the racial and ethnic make-up of our student population; perhaps we might even do better than our institutions do at creating a diverse and inclusive staff. Here are some ways we might accomplish that. Visit orientation sessions for incoming students of color. Ask tutors. They can be our best allies in recruiting a more diverse staff. Remind them to pay attention to our dedicated writing center users who have already proven through their actions that they are committed to the mission of the writing center; to the student in the residence hall who is a particularly focused listener; to the student government representative who is a careful responder. Finally, we can look to the vast expertise our tutors bring to the writing center. Is there a theater major on staff? How about turning him or her on to Augusto Baol's book, *Theater of the Oppressed* for exercises to address everyday racism.[7] Is there a music major on staff? How about asking that tutor to put together a presentation on world music or on white colonization of African-American music? We have also found a variety of ways to move this work out of the writing center as well. We have held campus-wide "Write up a Storm" fund-raisers for New Orleans schools. Our tutors have applied for and received student diversity grants to promote racial understanding. In short, given a pro-learning culture, the possibilities are limitless.

If we all, directors and tutors, recognize differences, as Kathryn Valentine has noted, "not simply to appreciate them but to draw on them as resources for making meaning and understanding the context in which we work and live" then the writing center will work, according to Valentine, "to facilitate students' ability to use diversity as a productive resource—as a resource for learning and representation, and not a characteristic which marks some of our students but not others."[8]

RACISM IS REAL 2: RECOGNIZING RACISM ACROSS OUR INSTITUTIONS

We note that one of the ways we might engage in anti-racism work in our writing centers is to broker considerations of race and racism across institutional boundaries. "Broker" is a word and a concept we take from Etienne Wenger, who writes that "[b]rokers are able to make new connections across communities of practice, enable coordination, and—if they are good brokers—open new possibilities for meaning" (109).

As the IWCA 2005 Summer Institute participants worked through stories of racism in small groups, they began to tell their own stories. Here is one of those:

> Raoul was a Latino tutor who had worked in the writing center for a year or so. During the course of a semester, it became evident to him, to all of the other tutors, and to the Director that a faculty member had warned his students not to work with Raoul. The faculty member had directed them fairly explicitly to work with the white tutors in the writing center. If you were this writing center director, what would you, as the broker, do? [9]

Having read our book to this point, you will realize that we are advocating a repositioning of the relationship that we, writing center directors, imagine (and maintain) between our institutions and ourselves. We are inviting you to think of yourself as a leader not only of your writing center, but also within your institution. Anti-racist leadership is difficult. We worry about what will happen to us if we begin to name racism when we see it. We might also begin to worry about what will happen to our writing centers. What is the right response to the faculty member who directs his students to avoid the tutor of color—the professor who seems incapable of recognizing and honoring the gifts, the leadership, the intelligence, the credentials of students of color?

One of the reasons, perhaps, that our fear of addressing racism—in this case, racial prejudice—handcuffs us is that we tend to imagine intervening as necessarily involving confrontation in a zero sum game. However, change-agent work can be approached in other ways. Many anti-racism activists advocate a change model that distinguishes between "transactional" change and "transformational" change. Transactional change is the model with which we are most familiar: it is confrontational, involves negotiation (you give me that and I'll give you this), or demands (you give me this or else) (2005 *Understanding and Dismantling Racism*). Transformational change engages other ways of thinking and acting. It is collaborative, process-oriented, holistic in the sense that it requires an attentiveness to the systemic and institutional context from which conflict emerges. Sound familiar? Sounds like writing center work, doesn't it? What happens in the boundaries between institutional sites, we wonder, when we begin to apply our core professional values, principles, and what we know of best practices in the writing center to anti-racism work across our institutions? Our individual experience suggests that disaster does not ensue. Instead, we've learned that what we know as writing center directors translates quite well to reflective leadership outside of our writing centers.

No one, we think, can or should do anti-racism work alone—the idea is oxymoronic. Look across your campus. Who are the people, which are the programs that are most likely to also be thinking and working on anti-racism? Faced with this situation, who could you go to for advice? Is there a faculty member in sociology who studies race and racism? Is there a director of multicultural studies who works regularly with faculty and students of color, and who might have encountered racism among the white faculty before? Who in administration seems most committed to diversity? We can take these people to lunch. Make friends. Forge alliances. Seek opportunities to collaborate with them.

Engaging in anti-racism work in the writing center requires, however, acknowledging the complexity of the racial order on our campuses. People of color may legitimately wonder at our motivations for beginning and may suspect our intentions and ability to follow through. People who direct programs for students of color across campus may legitimately wonder whether we are setting our program up in competition with theirs or seeking to exploit them or their programs. They may also legitimately wonder whether we have created and continue to create the conditions in the writing center necessary for the safety and meaningful support of students of color. These concerns are legitimate not because the writing center director, as an individual, is suspect, but because of a long, frustrating, and material history of white domination and appropriation of resources. These concerns are legitimate because of a long history of whites expecting or demanding assimilation from people of color rather than being willing to change themselves or to transform institutions built for whites and, at least in part, in service of racial domination. In their book, *The Miner's Canary: Enlisting Race, Resisting Power, Transforming Democracy*, Lani Guinier and Gerald Torres use the metaphor of the miner's canary to explain this last concern. Guinier and Torres suggest that education's response to the death and dying of the canary (students of color) is to try to change the canary, to resuscitate rather than to decontaminate the mine or build a new one.

Writing centers are deeply implicated, because of our traditional role as gatekeeper of academic literacy, in institutional efforts to change the canary. In fact, writing centers may be particularly susceptible to this phenomenon because of our traditional emphasis on working with individual students rather than on curriculum, faculty development, or institutional leadership, for example. As we noted earlier in this chapter, our focus on one-to-one instruction, while a trademark of writing centers, can get in the way of our ability to see this work as part of the institutional structures and hierarchies that enable racism to flourish on our campuses and may prevent us as well from embracing the writing center's potential in supporting anti-racism efforts cross-institutionally as well.

Not merely in spite of, but because of these challenges, we think the work is worth doing. Attempting anti-racism activism in and through our writing centers calls on our principles, our disciplinary knowledge, our particular orientations toward peer pedagogies as well as our creativity and our sense of wonder at the knowledge others possess and share.[10] Creating our writing centers as institutional spaces that depend on the presence, engagement, and histories of individuals within a diverse community and on an honest accounting of struggles for justice just might be, we think, a means by which we articulate and re-articulate the degree to which writing centers matter to our institutions and in the struggle for social justice.

Appendix

ANTI-RACISM WORK

DEFINITIONS OF RACISM

The following definitions come from a worksheet titled "Understanding and Naming Racism" and were developed for an anti-racism training for teachers in the St. Cloud, Minnesota school district. They are intended to give a sense of the complexity and ubiquity of modern racism, but also and more importantly perhaps, to provide language for naming those everyday experiences through which racism in individual and institutional forms circulates and reproduces.

Definitions

Racial Prejudice: Dislike, distrust, or fear of others based on perceived racial differences. Individual racial prejudice is learned and, at the early stages of anti-racist awareness, is often unconscious.

Racism: Racial prejudice in combination with community, institutional, and/or systemic power.

Institutional Racism: Visible and often invisible differential and unequal treatment of constituencies based on race. Inequalities with regard to access, power, and inclusion that are sanctioned by commission or omission by an institution.

Systemic Racism: The web of ideas, institutions, individual and collective practices that, taken together, ensure the perpetuation of social, political, and economic inequality along racial lines.

Manifestations

Unconscious or Unintentional Racism: Learned and deeply internalized racism that we carry with us through our days. Some part of our work as anti-racists is interior work: becoming conscious of our prejudices and actively working to transform ourselves. For example: feeling nervous or uncomfortable when encountering an individual or group of people from another perceived racial group.

False Attribution: The tendency to explain the actions or inactions of individuals or groups from perceived races other than our own in negative terms (while excusing our own actions or inactions). For example: assuming that a child of color is struggling academically because her parents are uneducated or uncaring or conversely assuming that academic excellence among children of color is anomalous (abnormal or unusual).

Triangulation: Assuming racial prejudices are shared among whites. For example: expressing negative, derogatory or racist views to other whites and assuming that they will all agree.

Unsolicited Nominations: Expecting or asking people of color to speak for their race.

Racialized Neglect: Providing unequal and inferior service, support, communication, and/or care to people of color. For example: calling on, praising, or offering academic enhancement opportunities to white children in a classroom with more frequency than children of color.

Racialized Gatekeeping: Actively or implicitly preventing or obstructing people of color from obtaining services, benefits, or privileges that are normally or regularly available to whites. For example: regular tracking of students of color into remedial courses or programs. Or making exceptions to regular practices or procedures for whites, but not for people of color.

Individual physical racial violence: Physical assault motivated by race.

Symbolic racial violence: Verbal assault motivated by race or racism communicated and reproduced through signs and symbols (for example: the association of black men with violence and hyper-sexuality through media representations in film, television, and print).

Group or community sanctioned violence: Physical and/or symbolic assault motivated by race and participated in or sanctioned by a group or community.

WHITE ANTI-RACISM

Based on Eileen O'Brien's sociological study of white anti-racist activists, *Whites Confront Racism: Antiracists and Their Paths to Action.* (Oxford: Rowman & Littlefield, 2001).

There are three main ways in which whites come to the work of anti-racism:

Activist Networks: Many whites are introduced to anti-racism through activist networks on a range of social and political issues.

Growing Empathy: Many whites come to anti-racism by developing empathy for people of color through a variety of "approximating experiences."

Turning Points: Many whites come to anti-racism through a turning point in their lives typically spawned by a dramatic or cathartic event.

Most white anti-racists will recognize some combination of the above factors that have drawn them to the movement.

O'Brien identifies three forms of "approximating experiences." These are experiences that enable whites to feel some understanding of what it must be like to experience racism as a person of color.

> *Overlapping Approximation:* Drawing analogies between racism and some form of oppression that a white person might experience (i.e. sexism or sexual violence).
>
> *Borrowed Approximation:* Witnessing racism as a close friend, lover, or family member of a person of color.
>
> *Global Approximation:* Noticing contradictions between strongly held ideals or democratic principles and the fact of racism.

Cautionary Notes About Empathy

One of the mistakes that many white anti-racists make is to assume that empathy is enough. Several critical race scholars have noted that comparisons and analogies between racism and other forms of oppression tend to disguise the disproportionate suffering of people of color under racism.

Also, white anti-racists sometimes also make the mistake of assuming that because they feel empathy, they actually do comprehend the lived experiences of people of color and are therefore qualified to speak on their behalf.

SHORT LIST OF READINGS

Aptheker, Herbert. 1992. *Anti-Racism in U.S. History: The First Two Hundred Years.* Westport CT and London: Greenwood Press.

Frankenberg, Ruth. 1993. *The Social Construction of Whiteness: White Women, Race Matters.* Minneapolis: University of Minnesota Press.

Frederickson, George M. 2002. *Racism: A Short History.* Princeton and Oxford: Princeton University Press.

Lipsitz, George. 1998. *The Possessive Investment in Whiteness: How White People Profit from Identity Politics.* Philadelphia: Temple University Press.

Omi, Michael and Howard Winant. 1994. *Racial Formation in the United States: From the 1960's to the 1990's.* New York: Routledge.

Rutstein, Nathan. 1993. *Healing Racism in America: A Prescription for the Disease.* Springfield MA: Whitcomb Publishing.

Sue, Derald Wing Sue. 2003. *Overcoming Our Racism: The Journey to Liberation.* San Francisco: Jossey-Bass.

Thandeka. 1999. *Learning to be White: Money, Race, and God in America.* New York: Continuum.

7

EVERYDAY ADMINISTRATION, OR, ARE WE HAVING FUN YET?

Between two evils, I always pick the one I never tried before.

Mae West

Do you lead like Gandhi? Bill Clinton? Mother Theresa? JFK? In developing scholarly arguments about administration and leadership for our manuscript, we stumbled on a very important data collection instrument: the Famous Leader Test.[1] We five took the challenge, and our results are listed above. (It will be up to you, reader, to guess which one of us is the sexually-charged glad-hander and which is the self-sacrificing martyr.)

While the leadership quiz did provide some comic relief during a particularly trying time of the semester, it wasn't all in fun, as it did bring to light some very real differences in the ways we lead in our professional lives and in the ways we theorize administrative work. The five of us didn't need the leadership quiz to point out that we are very different leaders, yet we seek out opportunities to enter a dialogue, to hear each other's rhetorics of the writing center. We are each other's sounding boards, ledge-talkers, backlist buddies, which leads us to wonder: What does Mother Theresa have to say to Bill Clinton? Or Gandhi to JFK?

If you lead like JFK, according to SimilarMinds.com, "you like power because it increases your sexual options; you are a thrill seeker by nature and you don't shy away from risky behavior." A Bill Clinton is a "social chameleon" who "likes[s] to be the center of attention and desire[s] fame." Mother Theresa's style, in contrast, is to "lead with your good works and helpful nature." A Mother Theresa leader is someone who "loves[s] to give."

None of us had much in common, apparently, with Albert Einstein, "a detached intellectual whose ideas saved/will destroy the world," or with Che Guevara, who has a "revolutionary artsy style." Apparently, "dying tragically on a mountain" doesn't appeal to us. And, though many of us in writing centers imagine that everyone is out to get us, no one scored a Hitler, who is "paranoid, . . . see[ing] threats everywhere and always focus[ing] on worst case scenarios." (Several of us, however, admitted to having responded to the following statement with a "Very Accurate" rating: "I have sometimes imagined dangers that did not really exist.")

LEARNING LEADERSHIP

Let's face it: We need each other to figure out how to do this particular job. Directing a writing center (and all that the job description entails) means extending our writing center learning culture (a deliberately created environment centered on learning) to include this community of practice we five have worked within (in fact, another learning culture). In doing so, we remain consistent with what Tagg calls a learning paradigm. Tagg sets this paradigm next to its antithesis, the *instruction* paradigm:

> In the instruction paradigm the mission of colleges and universities is to provide instruction, to offer classes. The successful college, by instruction paradigm standards, is the one that fills classes with students and thus grows an enrollment . . . the instruction paradigm has become not only the rules of the game in higher education but the lens through which many who work in colleges see their own institutions and their roles in those institutions. (15–17)

For Tagg, the problem with the instruction paradigm is that it focuses on delivery and transmission (through services or teaching) rather than on student learning. In contrast, the learning paradigm constitutes a set of practices aligned with "the mission of colleges and universities[,which] is to produce student learning. This end is primary; the means are secondary and are to be judged by how well they achieve the end" (31). Writing centers serve as one of the many "means" to that end—since we deploy multiple and alternative methods to make learning visible without direct measurement. What would writing center administration look like, and what kinds of philosophies and practices would we share, if we took Tagg's challenge seriously to remake our administrative practices to reflect this shift toward the learning paradigm?

When describing the differences between the learning paradigm and the instruction paradigm, Tagg reveals a set of actions that highlight the contrast between these "parallel theories" (15). Deep learning is associated with the learning paradigm, surface learning with the instructional. As with the learning culture audit we introduced in chapter four, the chart below is one way to take a look at how you view managing a writing center through the lens of learning. We follow Tagg's features and

TABLE 3

Learning Paradigm Audit

DEEP	SURFACE
Focuses on the signified; meaning of the text, problem, etc. *How can we best learn what that ESL student can teach us about learning a new language?*	Focuses on the sign; the surface appearance of the text, problems, etc. *Here comes that ESL student again; he is so demanding and difficult to understand.*
Active: learner is the conscious agent of understanding *How can we use the demand by the dean to increase usage by 30% to better teach the faculty and administration what we do, how we do it, and why we do it?*	Inert: learner receives what is given, remains static *Make more flyers and increase presentations in the residence halls.*
Holistic: learner sees how object of learning fits together and how it relates to prior learning *How can I write a report that connects the quantitative information that the administration values, with the qualitative analysis of our work, which we think speaks more authentically about what we do and its values?*	Atomistic: learner sees objects of learning as discrete bits of data *Include a chart that shows number of hours tutors worked and the numbers of students who were tutored.*
Seeks to integrate information into semantic memory *How can I encourage and support tutors in exploring old tutor journals and writing about how the new cohort of tutors views the issue?*	Generally stops with episodic memory *Everyone follows the same handbook from past years without question.*
Reinforces and is reinforced by incremental (developmental or constructivist) theory *How can I provide opportunities for tutors to talk about what they believed about their work when they started the job and what they would share with a newbie?*	Reinforces and is reinforced by entity (deficit learning) theory *Update personnel files for tutors and rehire the tutors who are good at getting to work on time.*
Reinforces and is reinforced by mindfulness *How can I provide group and individual opportunities for tutors to reflect on their writing conferences and talk about challenges, surprises, and new strategies without evaluation?*	Reinforces and is reinforced by mindlessness *Use the staff meeting to ensure that every tutor maintains a consistent approach in each session and that policies and procedures are followed.*
Experienced as enjoyable; open to flow experience *How can I support and validate tutors who work with one and another on their writing and research. How can I encourage them to independently explore their interests in tutoring and teaching writing?*	Experienced as unpleasant; closed to flow experience *The writing center is not a place where students can hang out, each lunch, or meet with each other when they are off-duty.*

Adapted from John Tagg: *The Learning Paradigm College*, page 81.

examples with writing center examples in italics. At the risk of reinforcing binaries, we tried to create examples that evoke possible writing center scenarios and by no means suggest that the chart captures every conceivable version of an event.

The chart prompted the five of us to reflect on how we have come to learn, to think about our teaching and student learning, and to realize again that we are not done. Just when we believe we've got it all figured out, we encounter situations in which our knowledge fails us. These moments present us with choices: should we bluff, run, lean in? Planting ourselves firmly in the learning paradigm offers greater opportunities to engage in deep learning when addressing new challenges of writing center leadership.

Few graduate programs offer explicit instruction in writing program administration; even fewer address the writing center director's need to both manage and lead. Jeanne Simpson (IWCA Summer Institute 2005) remarked that our field has been almost silent—neglecting to prepare future directors with even the most basic skills of administration. We agree with Simpson's assessment of the lack of managerial preparation. The skills we draw on, now that we have more or less settled into our professional identities, are complex. Yet as a field we have been remiss, in the silence that Simpson describes, in not looking to other kinds of successful leadership development models for guidance.

For example, with stunning regularity, voices clamor to a friendly online forum, the WCenter listserv, with pressing questions on writing center administration. The five of us have found kinship and mentoring on that list as well. We empathize with the perceived urgent need to do the right thing, but we've also discovered that a few well-intentioned email responses rarely solve the issue. Pre-packaged answers don't begin to drill into the complexity of most questions; the philosophical frame that supports those kinds of answers is rooted in the instructional paradigm: new challenges are seen as problems, and there is a drive for productivity and efficiency over learning. Once the dust settles on the WCenter listserv, questioners are often left to sort through fifteen or twenty separate responses, each of which raises a separate concern or highlights a different tangle. Most instructive, perhaps, is the lack of agreement on an appropriate course of action. The real work—that of putting these responses into dialogue with each other and figuring out how these responses intersect with one's institutional demands—is still left to do once subject lines have changed and a new crisis has taken the place of the old one. The questioner must still, in other words, learn to shape a leadership identity, one that accomplishes the managerial as well as the visionary.

We gather at Meg's kitchen table, or by telephone, by email, or at conferences in an effort to achieve both these aims: to accomplish the managerial and visionary in our leadership. The five of us found one another through both desire and need, not only for professional development or the resolution of the minutiae that affect our professional lives, but for affinity, friendship, stimulation. We share a passion for and commitment to certain ways of knowing and practicing what we are always coming to know. We are a "community of practice" with a transforming "domain" of knowledge that shapes emerging practices (Wenger et al 27). And in many ways, what we have learned from one another is to think of the managerial issues that emerge in the everyday as something more than problems to be solved in order that the real work of the writing center can be accomplished. This realization is a key feature of the philosophy we share. We have begun to conceive of these everyday challenges as moments of possibility in and through which we might more creatively manifest principles, create collaborative relationships, teach tutors, faculty, and our institutions with a richer accounting for the complexity of learning and producing knowledge in an intellectual community; and from these kernels of minutiae and management, the visionary grows. We may have turned to each other out of a sense of urgency, but what has developed is a sense of conviction about the power of a community of practice for committed professionals working in relative isolation. Together we have come to reject the idea that writing center directors wear different hats for different tasks, and to embrace instead a style of leadership through which interactions with writers, tutors, faculty, and administrators emerge from a common set of principles and a shared sense of goals.

Through this text, we've asked you to think about structural and functional leadership with us. Now we want to think about how structural and functional leadership intersect with the learning paradigm. How could we, as functional leaders, prompt deep learning across and beyond our campuses? Tagg believes the two types of leadership become more powerful as they merge. Structural leaders perform by virtue of where they exist within the structure, following a job description or title on the organization chart to the letter. This is not a bad thing; it is simply not all there is to leadership. Writing center directors who get good marks for running tight ships but never venture beyond to initiate projects or collaborate outside their primary spheres of influence are stranded on the structural leadership island. Functional leaders, on the other hand, extend their assigned role to move with mission and passion toward new challenges: they are compelled by an expansive sense of responsibility and broader vision, to collaborate for institutional change. Functional leaders will look for opportunities to partner with the libraries or the service learning coordinator or a local community group. No one right way merges these two forms of leadership. The challenge is to cultivate a mindfulness about which frame we are operating out of, and when, and why. Achieving that mindfulness does not mean, of course, that we have become the ultimate leader either; merging these types actually offers more opportunities for diverse leadership styles.

We can all be functional leaders in the effort to create a working community of practice around the issues of teaching and learning. The task of genuine leadership requires no special titles nor extended seniority. Every Learning Paradigm college will be a distinctive product of a living community of practice moving purposefully to realize its own vision of the Learning Paradigm. It is the central role of leadership to bring those communities to conscious action. (Tagg 340)

Just as we argue that tutors have been painted in the staff education literature as flat characters, as people who can rise above their individual writerly interests and scholarly preferences to become "standard" tutors, we view the writing center director's administrative options as having been similarly constrained. We tutor each other in alternative models of leadership, drawing on sources as diverse as Gallup organization reports, *Harvard Business Review* compendiums, books on stewardship and sustainability and Lance Armstrong's autobiography. Nothing is too far afield to be considered potentially useful—not even a crazy website appended to the bottom of an e-mail message, sent off as a joke.

Like you, we reject, in other words, the notion of a model writing center administrator and the idea that there is a "right" way to do this work. We revel instead in the everyday, in the recognition that a real leader leads from his or her own individual strengths and talents. For this reason, we do not fear the cult of personality that others have warned against. We acknowledge that our writing centers work in the ways they work because *we* work the ways *we* work. Understanding this observation involves teasing out the distinctions between leadership and administration. Many, like Che Guevera, lead without embracing the mantle of administrator, and we have been assured that, on occasion, there are those who administer (programs, universities, even entire nations—for more than one term!) without ever really *leading*.

One way to lead as well as to administer is to engage in and present our work as more than simply nuts and bolts. For example, many contemporary writing program administrators argue for developing theories of writing program administration in order to "advance and legitimate the claim that what we do is intellectual work" (Rose and Weiser 2). We view enacting this claim as consistent with practicing the "scholarship of teaching," a movement started by Ernest Boyer in *Scholarship Reconsidered* (1990). A recent iteration, the "scholarship of administration," is taken up by many, not just by writing program administrators; and Denise Doyle, a university vice president for academic and student affairs, notes that institutions that already demonstrate a "vibrant notion of what the scholarship of teaching and learning is, are more likely to draw the parallels to the work of administration" (7).

Such a vibrant notion involves recognizing that the realities of program development and maintenance do not afford us the ability to avoid the rush or the smudge of administrative work. Yet when we think of the ways writing center directors have been admonished to develop administrative strategies that assimilate to "central administration" in order to have our data "heard," or to "lean in," or to make a big noise about our budgets, our spaces, and our generally undervalued status, we are reminded of that strange stage in the rise of late 20th century feminism when the advice was: if you want to succeed like a man, you will need to dress like, eat like, talk like, deal like, cheat like, and boss like a man. We liken the adoption of these mannerisms to some misplaced concept of the "ideal" yet again, an accomodationist mentality that ignores our fundamental interest in, and talent for, teaching. As administrators on our campuses, should we assimilate, accommodate, or simply shut up?

We commonly hear the claim in our field, for example, that the most effective tool we have to create necessary and productive relationships with those we report to on the organizational chart is our rhetorical skill. We agree that many writing center directors are skilled rhetoricians, yet we are troubled by the assimilationist idea of this approach in the same ways that we are troubled by the all-too-familiar axiom about our role in bringing student writers to an understanding of or accommodation to the discourse of the academy. Without reiterating the arguments for and against this mission, suffice it to say that we think both types of assimilation promise little more than a way to fool others into thinking that you are doing what they want you to do by saying it the way they want you to say it.

That writing center directors sometimes believe ourselves more effective if we can "translate" our work to our institutions is an example of eliding Trickster. Hyde's other characterization of Trickster as treasonous/ translator reminds us of our fervent ferrying of information about our programs to "the other side" —upper or central administration, certainly somewhere most of us are not. The documents and data we prepare are often seen as more powerful if "translated" for this particular audience, yet at the same time we often feel queasy about our "treason." The better we do at translation, it seems, the more we are suspected of "going over to the dark side" or "selling out" to the administration. As traitors to our clan, we are caught in the middle: "[T]o translate is to betray . . . and the translator who connects two people always stands between them"

(Hyde 264). We wrestle daily with the inherent conflict between how what we do every day shapes and instantiates what we believe about student writers and how the institutional version of student writers continues to prevail. But consider the role of the writing center in systemic and institutional transformation. Maybe underneath many of the encounters with writers in the writing center is this question—or the assumption on our part—that our role is or should be so much more than receiving, accepting, and manifesting the values, traditions, and habits of mind and knowledge production that are identified and defined by others—the institution, the administration, the faculty. Remember why the Trickster moment is significant and important? Because it is in that moment that normalizing practices and the assumptions that underlie them are exposed not only in their absurdity, but also in their destructive power.

One director, Melissa Ianetta[2], admits:

> Quite frankly, I think one would be a bit of sucker not to learn the language of the administration: it's not that hard, and, judiciously used, it will make at least one of your audiences very happy. I do, however, believe that there's baggage that goes with any rhetorical model and that we need to think about that too. And it's a bummer if you figure this out the hard way. (Wcenter listserv: October 31, 2004)

RHETORICS OF LEADERSHIP

As we adopt a high-risk/high-yield approach to writing center pedagogy, we want to explore what it would mean to replicate high-risk/high-yield tactics in our leadership roles as well. By possessing the acumen to work with both upper administration and our writing centers and "embracing liminality"—as Melissa Ianetta suggests—we run the risk of facing an additional conflict: we are indebted to and held accountable by two different "certifying bodies." We must answer to our fellow writing center directors, as one "professional discourse community," and the institutions where we work, as another. Ianetta cautions that "a scholarly community of peers might value fluidity, encourage resistance to prescriptive norms, and reject positivist claims, but an institutional audience may well find such arguments unintelligible" (44). Nevertheless, in an email post to WCenter, Ianetta warns us not to ignore the limitations in adopting language strategies that "speak" only to administration:

> I don't believe that adopting the language of university administration is "just good rhetoric" as Jeanne [Simpson] suggests . . . I think adopting that

language of administration rests on the assumption that reality and rhetoric are separate things. Since I believe knowledge does not exist *prior* to language, but is constituted *in* language, I believe that using the terminology of administration changes the message. While the language of administration might provide common ground for a writing center and its administrative audience, it can also obscure what we do well.

Can we change the institutional perception of the writing center without changing the language we use to describe it? If we adopt the language of the faculty instead—or at least partially—and construct the writing center as a place of writing, teaching, AND research—or create new discourses that code the writing center as a place that "celebrates" writing, what persuasive paradigms do these new models offer us that the language of administration suppresses? Just as the language of marginalization / victimization affects how we define ourselves in some counter-productive ways, isn't the language of administration similarly limiting? (Wcenter listserv: October 31, 2004)

We champion an administrative rhetoric that celebrates not only writing, as Ianetta suggests, but a kind of teaching and learning that accomplishes its goals by saying less and doing more, in subversive and deliberate ways, as Cheryl Glenn describes in her book *Unspoken: A Rhetoric of Silence.* Even if we are inclined to believe less *is* more, this kind of strategic withholding runs counter to the academy, where "conversation has always been a medium for establishing oneself as an intellectual, social, or financial player" and silence becomes suspect, "perceived as emptiness"(Glenn 6, 75). From water cooler talk to formal annual reports, we are complicit in filling the gap with words that attempt to be recognized, accepted, and funded. If what Jeanne Simpson says is true—that "the kind of information that writing center directors will need to gather and distribute will not be as closely related to the philosophy and daily functions of a writing center as it will be to larger, institutional issues"(1995, 52)—then we are faced with a schism in our institutional work and in our professional identities. If we think of our institutions as the bosses or boss-communities to whom we are subject, of our discipline as composed by static and/or safe knowledge and practices to which we are bound, and of writing center administration as management narrowly conceived, then the schism appears to us to be intractable. These are not our only options, however. We can reframe by reminding ourselves and each other that our roles on our campuses are those of teachers and learners. As such, we can be administrators who participate in and shape learning cultures within institutions.

We admit, for example, that taking the Famous Leader Test and sharing the results began, functionally, as a way of beginning the writing process of this chapter. We laughed at the results—at the ways in which the iconic personalities the test affiliated each of us with both captured what we knew about ourselves and one another and revealed those faces of ourselves we attempt (and often fail) to hide in our professional lives. Perhaps each of us has retaken the Leader Test periodically, like we might retake the Meyers-Briggs Type Indicator, to see if we still exist or if there's any chance we've changed. But there is also a seriousness of purpose in our individual and collective efforts to drill deeper into what makes us tick as leaders. We are driven into the open spaces between certainty and chaos—into the unknown of our everyday lives as writing center directors—by curiosity, wonderment, a love of stories, the pleasure we take in laughter, as well as by fear, uncertainty, insecurity, and longing.

In this complex terrain, we've realized that our needs and desires do not lead us to the locus of all certainty about how a successful writing center ought to be run, how successful tutoring ought to be practiced, and how successful writing is produced. Rather, we are learning that the leadership principles and practices we value both emerge from and enable a sense of constancy about how our writing centers work. In other words, the five of us seek resonance and reverberation between the ways we work with our staff as learners, writers, tutors, and change-agents; the ways we work with our colleagues, faculty, administrators, and staff, across our institutions; and the ways we work with our colleagues across our profession, including one another. We're learning that our needs and desires as writing center directors may differ in degree but not in kind from those of our students and our colleagues. We're learning to value learning as a critical condition of writing center administration and of leadership.

So much, it seems to us, of what circulates as the how-to's of writing center administration—on WCenter and in other available forums—turns on foreclosing complexity so as to keep things running smoothly (by which we mean efficiently and with a minimum of confusion and/or interruptions or disruptions). Tutor in; writer in; writer out; tutor out. Paper better, writer smarter, evaluation positive, bean counted. Learning leadership, though, hinges on inviting the unknown into not only our tutors' and our colleagues' learning, teaching, writing lives, but into our own. And it is in the constancy of this practice—learning—that what we see as productive, incisive leadership is possible.

We've tried to be imaginative as we've talked about the writing centers on our campuses, and we've tried not to lose for ourselves the sense of learning that we wrote about valuing for our tutors in "Origami, Anyone?" One of us, for example, conceived of an anniversary video; collaborated with tutors, writers, and colleagues to create the video; and invited administrators into the writing center on the anniversary date for a screening. That video is now shown to incoming students at first year orientation and streams on the writing center website. More than one of us has combined joining assessment efforts on campus—writing pieces of accreditation reports, sitting on assessment committees—with collaborating with tutors who are facilitating their own focus groups or surveys of the writing center's services.

Rather than pinning our hopes for our leadership through the everyday on our ability to forecast and occlude the unexpected, we wonder how we might "collaborate with chance" (Hyde). When we encouraged our undergraduate staff to design writing center publicity posters, we were surprised to find that faculty chose a variety of posters to adorn their office doors. We would not have expected they would be as likely to choose "Cut the Bull" as they were to choose "Warning: A Weak Thesis May Be Harmful to Your Essay" and "No Plagiarism," but they surprised us.

A quick search of Amazon.com reveals over 30,000 titles listed under "leadership." As we read and write in our own discipline, we see that we are not alone in scanning the available literature for different leadership models. Joseph Janangelo, for example, draws on performance theory to offer an attractive concept in describing the possible role for the writing program administrator: *auteur*. In this model, individual creativity and risk seek outlets in continually redefining the work of the "director"—something we see as congruent with our emerging concepts of leadership outside the "major studio" tradition. What Janangelo finds useful in this metaphor is the ability to reconcile two elements of the enterprise, both commerce and art, while "helping us see our daily activities as opportunities for intellectual creativity rather than as a perpetually draining series of the 'usual [albeit vital] bureaucratic tasks'" (149). Likewise, Louise Wetherbee Phelps suspects the value of her course on writing program administration stemmed more from the ad hoc, improvisational, and intergenerational interaction than on the formal, didactic elements of the course. Phelps turns to Lave and Wenger's idea of a "learning curriculum" for leaders, one that "relies on the constitutive role in learning for improvisation, actual cases of interaction, and emergent processes that cannot be reduced to generalized structures" (35). This shift offers us a postmodern version of leadership, one which moves us away from a positivist approach that "focused on mechanisms of control" and toward a substantive approach, "involving the larger sense of meaning, mission, and identity of the organization as a whole" (Starratt 4).

In this context, what passes for the mundane in our writing centers may be precisely the site at which the disjunctions between our pedagogical principles and foundational hopes and dreams about our profession and our professional lives might be observed and parsed—not for resolution necessarily or cleaning up, but for learning more, in deeper, more satisfying ways. We might begin to see writing center leadership as intimately connected to the work of cultivating "leaderful organizations" within our writing centers, within our institutions, and across institutional lines. Together, we might work toward dynamic, edgy, abundant and sustainable growth of knowledge and practices.

LEADERFUL ORGANIZATIONS

Let's consider for a moment how and toward what ends we might engage our everyday tasks in service of constancy. Let's think about how we could use those everyday tasks to cultivate leaderful institutional culture. We suggest that, even as we make the most mundane decisions, we are teaching others—tutors, student-writers, colleagues, our institutions, and our profession—what we value about our work and, correspondingly, what it is that others should value about our work. Reporting documents (annual reports, self-study reports, assessment data) are prime examples of this premise. When we decide what and how we report, for example, we should ask ourselves whether we are reporting the things we want our institutions and our profession to value.

One common line item reported, for example, is the number of available writing center hours tutors actually spend tutoring on an annual basis. We will be the first to admit that none of our writing centers functions at 100% capacity, if that capacity is defined as every available hour filled with a tutor in a traditional session with a student-writer. But we would correspondingly argue that this data set is not a very useful performance measure. A goal of simply filling all available hours would be both fairly easy to attain and would at the same time tell us almost nothing about how well we are serving any of our populations. Reporting repeat visits, for example, would tell us more about whether students are finding our services helpful enough to make them want to return.

In contrast, reporting "open" hours automatically devalues much of the learning activities that we have advocated here: a tutor playing Scrabble with a nonnative speaker, for example; tutors doing research for a conference presentation; tutors talking with other tutors; or a staff member writing haiku for a staff development session. All of these activities are necessary to create and sustain the kinds of learning communities outlined in this book. Our point in this section is simple: Our institutional talk must mirror and support our center talk; our center talk must mirror and support our institutional talk. Much of the time spent carefully constructing and supporting learning communities in the writing center can be undermined with one ill-thought-out line on a spreadsheet. We shouldn't collect it just because we can, or because others do. Remember that looking at our work through the lens of the instructional paradigm reduces GM to making assembly lines, not cars.

For example, managing a budget is often seen as an administrative task. Anyone in control of a writing center budget has to figure out how many hours of writing center tutoring the available salary dollars will support for the academic year. This line item involves a simple calculation and seems absolutely straightforward. Devise the schedule, set up the payroll, input the data into Excel, and keep an eye on the figures as the year progress. Basic administration.

This salary line item, however, also offers opportunities for leadership on campus, especially if you worry (as we do) that your tutors are underpaid and/or if you would like (as we would) to be able to staff more hours annually. These opportunities extend beyond simply making an argument, in writing or at budget committee hearings, for increased salary dollars. They extend to the other areas on campus that rely on student expertise: lab facilities, research assistance, admissions offices, other tutoring services. We can find out what students are being paid elsewhere; determine whether supervisors in those areas have also been arguing for an increase; organize and consolidate efforts if it helps to make our case.

And this would be only a partial response to the salary line item. The rest of the response might involve working with admissions to identify potential tutors and capitalize on scholarship dollars, or working with financial aid to raise the minimum hourly wages for work study students selected as tutors. In all these cases, we would emphasize that working in these ways across campus does not involve working differently from the ways we work in our centers. We experience no jarring disconnect, no switching of hats, as we take these discussions into other venues. They are part and parcel of our work as writing center directors, not radical departures; they are everyday pedagogical opportunities where we both teach and learn; and they are leadership opportunities where we simultaneously work within and without our centers.

Don't Be Afraid

We do understand the pull to gather data on tutor productivity, narrowly conceived, or employ other standard performance measures: this data seems objective, and the antidotes to any failures revealed by the data seem attainable. We can imagine that if we market our writing centers differently or train our tutors differently or arrange our hours differently that in relatively short order every hour will be filled with just the right stuff, and we'll be done—ready to be recognized by our colleagues and our institutions for having attended to a knotty problem. Perhaps a kind of received greed is also at work in our desire to do good by wrapping questions of practice and productivity up into neat little packages. Our thinking in this regard may be connected to the cultural phenomena of desire—if only I get that new car, lose that ten pounds, then I'll be happy. If only every appointment were spoken for and my writing center served forty percent of my institution's students, then I could conceive of myself and be perceived as extraordinarily competent.

Here again, we are faced with the tension between Hochschild's real and potential selves. Underlying this culture of desire is, at base, a culture of fear: status anxiety, certification anxiety, performance anxiety. What will people think if they walk past the writing center and see a tutor making construction paper cutouts for a plastic dinosaur's mouth? What if the tutors talking with one another have their feet up on a writing center table, or what if they've gone outside to talk while they smoke? Is this an appropriate use of the institution's resources? Will I be perceived as less than rigorous in my own intellectual pursuits? Maybe people will stop recommending their highest-achieving students to be tutors in the writing center. Maybe the tutors will have no authority in their sessions with student writers. Maybe I'll have no authority in my meetings with the tutors. "Jane," as George Jetson would holler, "stop this crazy thing!!!!!!!"

This is, we suggest, the administrator's version of Tutorious Rex—the writing center super hero, imagined by our tutors, who knows all, guides all, solves all. What would be left for us to do, to strive for, or to learn if our desire for resolution of all questions or practices were attained? Most importantly, we wonder what message our neatly packaged data-bytes send about how we believe our work, the work of the writing center tutors, and the work of student writers is—or should be—valued by our institution and profession. And we wonder why we are so afraid to ask others to look inside our writing centers with us to see what they might not have imagined seeing.

In a session on writing center leadership at the 2005 International Writing Centers Association Summer Institute for Writing Center Directors and Professionals, [3] Jeanne Simpson and Frankie Condon asked participants to identify the range of fears that might prevent us from capitalizing on our impulses to act as leaders or to enact our values across our institution. Jeanne and Frankie cajoled participants to go toward those things we fear rather than constructing ways to avoid doing what makes us anxious. We know that student writers and our tutors feel fear and anxiety around their various labors in and through the academy. Although our colleagues' fears are perhaps more deeply concealed in professional personae, we can recognize, if we are attuned to do so, the degree to which the choices they make or refuse to make might be informed by fear. The challenge for us as writing center directors, as administrators and leaders, is to engage with our own fears without being disabled by them—and to teach the value of that engagement both inside and outside the writing center.

While many of us have integrated technology into our writing centers' daily operations, others of us fear technology. We think it may take us away from what we are committed to: one-on-one, face-to-face tutoring. We think we don't know enough about it to use it well. We resist it. But rather than resisting technology, blindly accepting it or having it forced upon us, we might begin to use it for our own interests and as a part of the learning cultures we're developing in our writing centers. One of us, in a technologically challenged writing center, feared that any move to integrate technology might become a time sink, but technology teaching grants seemed too good an opportunity to resist. We were reminded that such a grant doesn't have to draw us into work we didn't intend to do. Reconceived, such a grant can entice others to be more intrigued in the work we are already doing in our writing centers. So now a grant supports an iPod project, and tutors reflect on their conferences by recording them with their own everyday technology. Perhaps these tutors will eventually teach faculty from their mini-research projects. Certainly, we will be teaching others on campus about the work of the writing center as soon as we're awarded grants like this one.

Mattering and Marginality

In our collaboration on this book, each of us has at different times and in a variety of ways wondered about the quality of our contributions, wondered when the others will discover that we don't really belong around the kitchen table, or learn how little we know and how foolish we are. Threading through our process is this strand: that the presence and becoming of each of us matters to the whole, even though singly none of us could have produced the whole. As collaboration on projects like this can teach us much about our mutual contingency, so our writing centers stand to teach students, tutors, faculty and staff colleagues, and our institutions about the value of the relational, of shared need, to intellectual communities or learning organizations. This potential can only be realized, however, to the extent that we are willing to share responsibility (and credit) for success, to risk failure, to laugh at our failures, foibles, and fears, and to show the public face of learning.

This aspect of the cultivation of learning leadership might be termed "mattering"—the antithesis of a term familiar to writing center professionals: marginality. According to Nancy Schlossberg,[4] environments that foster mattering can counter marginality; in these places you can see "mattering is a motive and does determine behavior" (11). Once found significant, students, staff, and faculty feel more connected and involved with their collective higher education. Thus, one of the necessary conditions both for individual and organizational learning is a shared conviction that one's presence, one's engagement, and one's contributions matter. We know from experience that we are able to be challenged and to learn from moments of challenge in nearly direct proportion to the degree that we are affirmed, welcomed, assured that we matter and that we do in fact have something of value to teach.

In *First Break All the Rules: What the World's Greatest Managers Do Differently*, authors Buckingham and Coffman undertake a Gallup organization study of more than 80,000 managers at 400 companies. Analyzing survey responses from over 105,000 employees, the authors identify six survey questions that correlate most highly with the greatest number of successful business outcomes. The six questions are as follows:

1. Do I know what is expected of me at work?
2. Do I have the materials and equipment I need to do my job right?
3. Do I have the opportunity to do what I do best every day?

4. In the last seven days, have I received recognition or praise for my good work?

5. Does my supervisor, or someone at work, seem to care about me as a person?

6. Is there someone at work who encourages my development? (33–34)

When we began discussing this study, we five were struck by how applicable the telling questions were to our own workplaces. They suggest to us that the administrative discussions in our field don't have to be—indeed, perhaps shouldn't be—focused on efficiency, policies, and programs, on "adopted" rhetoric or the whims of "central administration." These discussions should center instead on what many seem to fear, even as we know this focus is our strength: individual people. The best managers, according to Buckingham and Coffman, recognize talent broadly conceived; and those managers cater to the individual talents of their employees, rather than try to downplay those talents in some misguided attempt at consistency (71).

Having read Buckingham and Coffman, we were not surprised, then, when a panel of tutors in a Q & A session at the 2005 IWCA Summer Institute for Writing Center Directors and Professionals cited the potential impact of their work—the ability, in other words, to make a real difference to people—as the best thing about their writing center jobs. And we heard them loud and clear when they also noted that they would like their good work to be recognized more often (see question 4 above). They were articulating the importance of mattering and reminding us that practicing mattering is one of the most significant gestures we can offer in our own roles.

We can practice mattering in all sorts of ways. We might begin, for example, by expanding our definition of what makes a good tutor. Most of us probably don't think about our recruitment strategies as opportunities to practice mattering; but if those strategies lead us to pull from the same small percentage of students each year—the honors students, the "best" writers, the "grammar" aces—then we have narrowed our definition of talent in a way that may well be at odds with the message we want to send about the value of diverse intellectual contributions. Talent, as Buckingham's and Coffman's managers define it, is "a recurring pattern of thought, feeling, or behavior that can be productively applied" (71). Understanding talent in this way should cause us to look again at the tutor who can't sit still, the tutor who never managed to speak up in class, the tutor who doodles on whatever surfaces she can find. Our job is to expand our understanding of the writing center so that all of these tutors can fit. Then our message in the center will be consistent with our message across campus: There is a place for you here in our writing center; you belong. If we can't figure out ways to acknowledge our tutors' belonging, complete with all their quirks and idiosyncrasies, then we shouldn't be surprised if they can't figure out how to help students belong.

Sometimes helping students belong means recognizing their risk-taking. After attending a half-day workshop on art and writing, we asked Nikki and Missy, two tutors who were Secondary Ed./English majors, if they'd like to go to a week-long course offered for teachers in a neighboring state's public school system. They agreed, even though they would be the only undergraduates and the only people not from that state. They took on new roles as brokers for their own learning and for their home community of practice. As Wenger tells us, "The job of brokering is complex. It involves processes of translation, coordination, and alignment between perspectives" (109). The complexity of their position became most notable during the day, when they often felt "othered" by the group that was primarily concentrating on art and writing in the classroom. But every night they had long discussions with each other about the ways in which what they were learning might be applied to tutoring.

The two worked out the connections, but when, back home, with excitement, Nikki and Missy introduced what they'd learned, they met skepticism from the other tutors. "This is a lot of fun, but I don't see how it will work in tutoring." "I'm not artistic." "It probably won't work for me." The beginner's mind balked at the unfamiliar—not so different from the beginning writers who use the writing center. "I love writing poetry, but I hate writing papers." "I'll probably get another F." "I can't write." Sound familiar? Rather than being discouraged, though, the two tutors kept at it. Wenger tells us that brokering "requires enough legitimacy [on the part of the brokers] to influence the development of a practice, mobilize attention, and address conflicting interests. It also requires the ability to link practices by introducing into a practice elements of another" (109). Since these tutors were seasoned practitioners, the others recognized that legitimacy and were willing to participate. Over the course of several months, we and the tutors played with drawing to access writing, and writing to access drawing-to-access-writing. We read poetry and drew. We drew and wrote poetry. Still, although people were finding the work enjoyable, no one tried to use art in tutorials.

There was more discussion of how art and tutoring might go together; rolls of white paper covered the tutoring tables, with jars of crayons, markers and paints on each. Instant availability of the tools seemed important, but it took continual practice to tie drawing to tutoring at the bi-weekly meetings, to bring the others into the practice. Little by little, evidence of mapping, diagrams, and sometimes drawings emerged on the paper-covered tables. Finally, after a semester, there were the first full-fledged art and writing tutorials. One session ended with the writer carefully cutting out the drawing to take it with her. Another session was more involved. The assignment? "Your creative task is to develop a totally unique and creative design and layout for an automobile display window. You must accomplish this by using the preinventive form of a puzzle." The student was also directed to include the "metacomponential strategies" that she used. Monika, her tutor, immediately suggested drawing. In her pre-writing, the student lists the strategies she used: "Writing center, magazines, and TV. In the writing center, talk, ideas, brainstorming, and a visual picture." The student generously shared with us all of the artifacts of her writing center work—six or so pages of sketches of cars, of cars as puzzles with questions and comments, and lists interspersed throughout.

In the meantime, we and the tutors (prematurely, it turned out) offered workshops in art and writing to the first year composition faculty. They presented four. Two were utter failures, and two were very successful. It so happens that the successful workshops were easily connected to what was happening in the classroom. In one case, the instructor was asking students to "read" photographs, and in the second, the students were studying artifacts as part of the field studies they were writing. In the other two classes, the workshop was a stand-alone activity, and most of the students couldn't see how they might use art as a way into writing. Big surprise? No, it mirrored the tutors' initial reactions and early experiences with Nikki's and Missy's idea; this type of learning takes time, context, and reinforcement.

This story reflects two elements of our call for more leaderful organizations: first, supporting new experiences for our tutors beyond our centers—showing them that they "matter"; and second, envisioning ways to develop "brokers" and ambassadors to bring those new experiences to bear on other teaching and learning environments on our campuses.

Yet we also need to be planning for what "matters" in the future, as Jeanne Simpson and Michele Eodice demonstrated at the 2005 International Writing Centers Association Summer Institute for Writing

Center Directors and Professionals. Distributing a scenario to the participants in which a pleased parent donates $3000 to the writing center, Jeanne and Michele asked the participants individually and in groups to make decisions about how to spend that money. Fairly quickly, most of the groups decided that spending it on salary was not the best use of the money, since it would not be in the budget in subsequent years. From there, several groups had extended conversations about renewable resources, and discussion turned to the purchase of resources that would last the longest—often equipment or technology purchases. Another renewable use to which this money might be put would be to spend it on staff development. Participants and leaders at several tables did discuss this option, and several wondered about the advisability of this choice. A conference might last, they thought, for three or four days. Then the money would be gone, they explained, the tutors would be home, and what kind of lasting effect would the spent money have on the life or work of the writing center? We assert that spending money in this way might be a mattering practice: an investment of belief and encouragement in individual tutors, but also an act of cultivation in growing and promoting a learning culture in which tutors producing, sharing, and studying knowledge and best practices is highly valued.

Leadership Matters

We often hear directors talk about the divide between their inside-the-center work and their efforts to reach out, mesh with, and be supported by the institution. Particularly with regard to directors' work with faculty, we hear frustration and isolation. Michele Eodice, in her essay "Breathing Lessons or Collaboration Is . . .", writes that "when asked, many writing center directors will say that their peer relations, their relationships with their institutions, their identity politics, are anything but collaborative" (115).

Eodice goes on to suggest that "a set of tropes continually deployed to describe our relationships and positions in our institutions forecloses on possibilities of uncovering (and thus *teaching*) what undergirds both our tangible daily practice and our abstract desire: collaboration" (115). We suggest here that the intellectual creativity necessary for leadership within our centers can be harnessed for our work with the larger institution. The recovery of, advocacy for, and practice of the collaborative outside of our writing centers constitutes a rich opportunity to fold into our writing centers ideas or substances that might enrich and inform our thinking as tutors, directors, and scholars. Concomitantly, creating and sustaining the collaborative in our interactions outside of the writing center opens opportunities for us to teach and for others to learn the value of the ways we think and work within the writing center and how these approaches might enrich our colleagues' teaching and learning lives as well as our institutions. You will be recognized as the director of the writing center as you walk across your campus; this is you as structural leader. But imagine when that role merges with the functional leader in you:

> For the community to thrive, the members must participate in negotiating the living meaning of their practice, testing the artifacts of their history against the daily application of purposes to problems. The leader's role is to facilitate that participation and to elicit it where it is not forthcoming. (Tagg, 337)

In fact, to lead as we're suggesting, perhaps we must all believe that our leadership matters just as much beyond our writing centers as it does in our writing centers, that our leadership is creating change deep within and well beyond our institutions' walls even as we manage our budgets, report on our writing centers' activities, market the writing center, and hire, supervise and mentor our tutors. This sense of our own leadership, this sense that we can create change and nurture learning communities/communities of practice may be even more important in the world we are living in today. Terry Tempest Williams thinks so. She asks us to think seriously about what she calls "the open space of democracy," a space in which there is "room for dissent" and "room for differences," a space where "cooperation is valued more than competition," and the humanities are not peripheral, but the very art of what it means to be human" (8). Noting that we are living in a time with an "escalation of rhetoric" and fear, in which "force has trumped debate and diplomacy" (2), Williams argues that "democracy invites us to take risks. . . . It asks that we vacate the comfortable seat of certitude, remain pliable, and act, ultimately, on behalf of the common good" (22).

Williams pushes us to speak and act, to lead strongly, but she also reminds us that we must listen, for "we are nothing but whiners if we are not willing to put our concerns and convictions on the line with a willingness to honestly listen and learn something beyond our assumptions. . . . If we cannot do this . . . we will be left talking with only like-minded people" (22). "To commit to the open space of democracy," Williams asserts, "is to begin to make room for conversations that can move us toward a personal diplomacy" (23): "Do we dare to step back—stretch—and create an arch of understanding?" (24). Consider the everyday situations in which we might need to or could create this arch of understanding through conversation: defending the writing center in public forums, in front of those who say, "If they can't write, they don't belong in college"; planning large scale faculty development workshops that challenge deeply-held institutional attitudes and biases; collaborating with our colleagues on issues of diversity or access; learning (happily) that a colleague's work intersects with our own academic interests and finding out at the same time (unhappily) that same colleague didn't even realize we had a research agenda. Suddenly, we have the opportunity to explain our interests even as we hear about the interests of another.

Yet we miss opportunities to construct that arch of understanding too. Consider how many of us have been stopped in a hallway to garner yet another "atta boy" from a faculty member? Hearing "What you do is so great . . . I appreciate what you do" may sound like they "get it," but what follows can be disturbing: "Thank god you are working with these students. No one else would. You really take the heat off of us." A first reaction: anger, a reddening face, a false politeness that masks rage and frustration. But what if any one of us could take this encounter as an opportunity to assert our leadership by seeing another way into the conversation? How about a response like this: "Faculty are an important part of our work. This is a partnership to help students see that everyone here is a writer. We depend on you too, to talk with students about their writing, to demonstrate that you care about their improvement, to offer feedback and share your own stories of success and challenge with writing." Each of us might say this in a slightly different way, but we might all begin to see a moment like this one, and all of our moments of challenge, as moments of possibility and moments where mattering might make all the difference, and we might find we don't need to talk only with those who are like-minded. It's also not just a writing center director who can or should create these arches of understanding. Remember our learning culture audit from "Origami, Anyone?" In a "pro-learning culture," everyone listens, suggests, shares stories, experiments, explores, learns and participates.

———

So what *does* Mother Theresa have to say to JFK? Or Bill Clinton to Gandhi? Quite a lot, as it turns out, if we allow those conversations to begin. As Bill Clinton and George Bush (the first one) have

NOTES

PREFACE

1. For a discussion of co-authorship naming devices, including first author strategies and graphic representations of writing partnerships, see *(First Person)²: A Study of Co-Authoring in the Academy*, Kami Day and Michele Eodice, (Utah State University Press, 2001), especially pages 118–119.

2. These ideas come from a workshop offered at Clark University, September 14, 2006: *Difficult Dialogues Project Faculty Workshop*. The consultants: The Ashland Institute 2006. Barbara Tecil and Teri Chickering.

CHAPTER ONE: INTRODUCTION

1. We will use the term *tutor* to describe what most of us in writing centers recognize as the universal term for peer tutor in writing. We acknowledge that a variety of terms are now in wide use, such as *writing consultant, writing assistant, writing coach*, etc.

2. The field of organizational leadership teems with books to appeal to every type of management style or workplace. We have found that many writers who study practices in business, such as Etienne Wenger and Peter Senge, can be applied usefully in educational settings.

3. See, for example, the work of Nancy Grimm, Elizabeth Boquet, Victor Villanueva, and Nancy Welch, for useful challenges to our assumptions about writing center work.

4. Max Depree, former CEO of Herman Miller Inc., published *Leadership is an Art* (1990) and *Leadership Jazz* (1993). Richard Borden quotes DePree in his article "The Art of Deanship" (*Chronicle of Higher Education*, July 8, 2005).

5. We have been inspired by the work of Myles Horton, William Ayers, and Kirk Branch, all of whom believe we should keep our "eyes on the ought to be." Richard E. Miller, too, explores possibility in the face of crisis in *Writing at the End of the World*:

   > Why go on teaching when everything seems to be falling apart? Why read when the world is overrun with books? Why write when there's no hope of ever gaining an audience? Posing such questions aloud is not a sign of despair; it's a way to start a conversation about how and why reading, writing, and teaching the literate arts can be made to continue to matter in the twenty-first century. Schools currently provide extensive training in the fact that worlds end; what is missing is training in how to bring better worlds together. (x)

CHAPTER TWO: TRICKSTER AT YOUR TABLE

1. For a concise explanation of the Trickster/Coyote motif in myth, see: http://www.geocities.com/opzel57/coyote72.html
   Also, see Larry Ellis, "Trickster: Shaman of the Liminal" (*SAIL: Studies in American Indian Literatures*, Series 2, 5.4, Winter 1993), 55–68. http://oncampus.richmond.edu/faculty/ASAIL/SAIL2/54.html#55

2. Michael Webster at Grand Valley State University teaches courses on world mythology and writes about Tricksters: http://faculty.gvsu.edu/websterm/Tricksters.htm.

3. From a Web resource: *Axel's American Indian Page: Legends and Myths* http://www.axel-jacob.de/legends.html

Michael Spooner, in "Too Many Books: Sampling on the Subject of Publish-or-Perish in Composition," (*Writing on the Edge*, 15.1 Fall 2004) weaves a Coyote tale through his own take on"losing our eyes." In composition, he points out, the value we place on publication collides ironically with the publishing house practice of giving away rhet/comp books for free at scholarly conferences.

4.   *Technical rationality* generally refers to a paradigm of viewing the world (schools and teaching especially) from a positivist stance. From art professor, Alina Hughes http://www.adgd.net/documents/ahughes-teachingdesign.pdf:

> "Technical rationality" is concerned with finding best means to predetermined ends, on the assumption that higher quality processes lead to higher quality products. This model fits the modular system currently favoured in higher education and its orientation towards "rational management." By contrast, the "competent practitioner" approach demands that the process being undertaken by such a practitioner is critically and dynamically reassessed whilst actually taking place. Its promoters maintain that this is the single most important tool to offer future professionals in rendering them capable of dealing with the unexpected aspects of real practice.

5.   It might be time to assert our understanding of the differences between *training* and *educating*. From a variety of fields, we see professionals compelled to make clear these distinctions. Harold Jarche (in *Training vs. Education (but its all learning)* http://www.jarche.com/node/189) writes:

> Training, such as how to drive a car, can use a more scientific method to optimize training time, achieve the desired performance and reduce the risk of accidents. Training and education can even use the same tools, like simulations, but not the same approach. Education and training are complementary, but distinct.

One writer discusses the use of blogs (training students to use them vs. learning what can be done with them). And, in another area, computer science, the lament is: "There must be a balance between memorizing procedures and understanding concepts." http://www.virtualbill.net/cc/
In *Workplace Learning for the Coming Century*, (http://www-tcall.tamu.edu/erica/docs/harris/harris4.pdf) Lawrie (1990) identified training as a "change in skills" whereas learning was defined as "a change in knowledge" (44). Rothwell and Sredl (1992) believed that "training is a short-term learning intervention intended to establish—or improve—a match between present job requirements and individual knowledge, skills, and attitudes" (4). Education, in their view, "is an intermediate-term learning intervention intended to help individuals qualify for advancement and thus achieve their future career goals" (5).
And the NASAS Office of Logic Design claims to educate design engineers, not train them. In their words, "Training promotes rote responses. Education promotes thinking and the ability to adapt to and cope with new situations." (http://klabs.org/mapld04/tutorials/vhdl/presentations/introduction.ppt#3)

6.   Friends of the *Writing Center Journal* Blog started up in 2004 to offer readers an opportunity to read posts from current authors and to discuss in more depth issues raised by articles in the journal. Ramsey's post on March 28, 2005 relates to the WCJ article "The Polyvalent Mission of Writing Centers" which was written with Phillip Gardner. (http://writingcenterjournal.blogspot.com)

7.   Google Glossary defines bricoleur. (http://www.bricoleur.org/archives/000033.html)

CHAPTER THREE: BEAT (NOT) THE (POOR) CLOCK

1. See *Teaching in the Rhythms of the Semester* for a fuller discussion of this concept.
2. Donald Murray (1968) says: "I find it helpful to have a clock where I can see it but where the student cannot see me looking at it. Conferences should probably be scheduled for ten minutes each, although most conferences will take only three or four minutes" (150). Murray does go on to say that this is possible because the teacher would already be familiar with the student's writing and so "does not need hour-long get-acquainted sessions" (150). See also Murray, Donald M. "The Listening Eye: Reflections on the Writing Conference." In Graves, *Rhetoric and Composition* (Upper Montclair, NJ: Boynton/Cook, 1984), 263–268.
3. See, for example, Robert Levine (1997) and Anne Ellen Geller (2005).
4. "Since taking up speed golf, Smith has seen his own scoring average in regular rounds of what he now calls 'slow golf' drop from 74 or 75 to below 72." (http://speedgolfinternational.com/articlebenefits.htm, June 15, 2005)
5. "Seat time" refers to how much time (fungible/mechanical time) we are forced to spend in school. The 180-days-in-school-chairs model. *Prisoners of Time: Report of the National Education Commission on Time and Learning* (http://www.ed.gov/pubs/PrisonersOfTime/index.html April 1994)

CHAPTER FOUR: ORIGAMI ANYONE?

1. Suggestions on how to maximize your learning culture are available in Clawson and Conner 2004. For more information on the audit, see the Web site: http://www.agelesslearner.com/assess/cultureaudit.html
2. We simply suggest being aware of the many types of barriers to recruitment and retention of diverse writing tutors. For example, program tracks with predetermined course offerings may mean that students who work full-time cannot arrange their schedules to accommodate honors classes, thus losing an opportunity to contribute in that environment. Also, high-achieving students of color may decide that they don't want to be the only representatives of their race in every class.
3. Initials are: http://www.montreat.edu/tutor/
4. *The Peer Writing Tutor Alumni Research Project* is one such place; this archive of data about what our former peer tutors are doing now can tell us much about what can be learned in a writing center (http://www.marquette.edu/writingcenter/PeerTutorAlumniPage.htm).

CHAPTER FIVE: STRAIGHTEN UP AND FLY RIGHT

1. From a review of Yancey's keynote in *Across the Disciplines:*

> Yancey laid the foundation for curricular change by relating the growth of a reading public in the 19th century with a new *writing* public in the 20th and 21st centuries. This writing public is forming in response to new possibilities afforded by information technologies, in particular blogs, email, instant messaging, listservs and other discussion forums, and the multi-genred texts that are emerging to support communities that form across the boundaries of location, class, and ethnicity. Most important, it is a writing public that is writing outside the academy and without our instruction. Members of the writing public, noted Yancey, "need neither self assessment nor our assessment: they have a rhetorical situation, a purpose, a potentially world-wide audience, a choice of technology and medium—and they write. Our model of teaching composing, as generous, varied, and flexible as it is in terms of aims and as innovative as it is in terms of pedagogy—and it is all of these—(still) embodies the narrow and the singular in its emphasis on a primary and single human

relationship: the writer in relation to the teacher," said Yancey. This model is not consistent, she said, with the development of a writing public in which collaboration within and across communities is the norm. Nor is our focus on print-based academic genres consistent with the development of documents that employ multiple genres and multiple media. Instead, she said, our current model privileges "a singular person writing over and over again—to the teacher." (Mike Palmquist. "Review: Keynote Address— 'Made Not Only in Words: Composition in a New Key,' by Kathleen Blake Yancey," http://wac. colostate.edu/atd/reviews/cccc2004/ April 15, 2004.)

2.   The cost of room, board, and tuition at Fairfield University, a private Catholic college in Connecticut.

3.   For samples of tutor-produced films, visit the University of Kansas writing center website at: www.writing.ku.edu. The video on this main page was developed with students, tutors, faculty, and staff for the whole campus to view. Another tutor produced film celebrated the five year birthday of the center, www.writing.ku.edu/gallery, and a mock interview with Roland Barthes can be found at: www.ou.edu/writingcenter/barthesinterview.html

4.   What we also included in the chapter epigraph. See Spellmeyer 1996.

CHAPTER SIX: EVERYDAY RACISM

1.   Statistics are not available, but our hunch is that racial and ethnic diversity among writing center directors (let's say, of the almost 1,000 of us out there) is not representative of the diversity in the population at large or in the percentage of racial and ethnic diversity existing among our students. We are also represented by a very white organization International Writing Centers Association (IWCA), and, like most of the "caring professions" such as teaching, positions are filled predominantly by female professionals.

2.   In fall 2005, Victor Villanueva performed a memorable keynote at the IWCA Conference in Minneapolis, Minnesota. The theme for his talk was on the writing center's role in anti-racism work and has since been published ("Blind: Talking About the New Racism" in *Writing Center Journal* 26.1:3–19). For weeks following the conference, the WCenter listserv was the site of a lively exchange regarding what role white writing center directors could play in recruiting diversity and actively engaging in campus anti-racism work.

3.   *The Mirror*, volume 20, issue 26, p. 1. This is the campus newspaper for Fairfield University in Fairfield, Connecticut.

4.   The concept of racism as individual race-based prejudice expressed in its most extreme forms as racially motivated violence (a dictionary-definition as it were) fails to account for a more complex understanding of racism's subtler and more widespread—and more profoundly entrenched—forms (institutional and systemic racism). See Judith Katz for an early example of this definition: *White Awareness: Handbook for Anti-Racism Training* (Norman and London: University of Oklahoma Press, 1978), 7–21.

5.   For a fuller discussion of the term "tutor training," see Boquet's *Noise from the Writing Center* (Logan, UT: Utah State Univ Press., 2001). We use the term "staff education" rather than "tutor training" in order to signal a shift to a more ongoing and holistic orientation to writing center work, which could include a variety of workshops, credit-bearing, non-credit bearing courses, a regular practicum, retreats, etc.

6.   We adapted the privilege audit from Peggy McIntosh's "White Privilege: Unpacking the Invisible Knapsack" (2005). Original source: Working Paper 189. "White Privilege and Male Privilege: A Personal Account of Coming To See Correspondences through Work in Women's Studies" (1988), by Peggy McIntosh; available for $4.00 from the Wellesley College Center for Research on Women, Wellesley MA 02181 The working paper contains a longer list of privileges. And a version found online:

http://seamonkey.ed.asu.edu/~mcisaac/emc598ge/Unpacking.html

7. Boal, a contemporary of Paulo Freire, advocates theater as a site for intervention in and exploration of oppression. He writes,

> We are used to plays in which the characters make the revolution on stage and the spectators in their seats feel themselves to be triumphant revolutionaries. Why make a revolution in reality if we have already made it in the theater? But that does not happen here: the rehearsal stimulates the act in reality. Forum theater, as well as these other forms of a people's theater, instead of taking something away from the spectator, evoke in [him] a desire to practice in reality the act he has rehearsed in the theater. The practice of these theatrical forms creates a sort of uneasy sense of incompleteness that seeks fulfillment through real action." (141–142)

8. Kathryn Valentine raised this issue in her Conference on College Composition and Communication 2005 talk entitled "'Diversity' and Tutor Education at a Hispanic-Serving Institution."

9. This scenario comes from several used in a workshop at the 2005 International Writing Centers Association Summer Institute by Harry Denny and Frankie Condon. Denny contributed this scenario from an actual event in his writing center at SUNY Stony Brook.

10. Several of us heard Emily Hall, from the University of Wisconsin-Madison, make this point compellingly during her Conference on College Composition and Communication 2005 presentation "Examining the Construction of Whiteness in Tutor Training."

CHAPTER SEVEN: EVERYDAY ADMINISTRATION OR ARE WE HAVING FUN YET?

1. A disclaimer from SimilarMinds.com, a web amusement:

> SimilarMinds.com is a resource for personality tests and personality psychology. Currently, there are a number of personality tests online (Enneagram test, Advanced Enneagram, Compatibility test, Jung, Big 5, Word Association, and others). There is also Ask The Oracle which is a decision making tool.
> All the tests at SimilarMinds.com are developed based on scientific measures used to ensure test validity. Multiple statistical measures are used to ensure test questions measure what they are intended to measure. Some of the free tests are experimental versions but even those tests are made up of pre-tested and validated questions.
> (http://similarminds.com/leader.html)

2. Melissa Ianetta, writing center director at the University of Delaware, gave us permission to quote from her email posts to the WCenter listserv.

3. The Summer Institute for Writing Center Directors and Professionals is a week-long intensive workshop offered each summer. In 2005 the Institute was hosted by the University of Kansas. For more information on the IWCA Summer Institute see: www.writingcenters.org. The most recent SI at the time of this writing was held at Stanford: http://swc.stanford.edu/iwcasi2006/index.htm.

4. For an introduction to the idea of "mattering," which is a term used primarily within the student personnel, student support services, or student affairs literature, see Nancy K. Schlossberg, "Marginality and Mattering: Key Issues in Building Community" in D.C. Roberts (ed.) *Designing Campus Activities to Foster a Sense of Community*. New Directions for Student Services, no. 48. (San Francisco: Jossey-Bass, Winter 1989.)

REFERENCES

Babcock, Barbara A. 1984. Arrange Me Into Disorder: Fragments and Reflections on Ritual Clowning. In *Rite, Drama, Festival, Spectacle: Rehearsals Toward a Theory of Cultural Performance*, ed. John J. MacAloon. Philadelphia: Institute for the Study of Human Issues, Inc.

Bluedorn, Allen C. 2002. *The Human Organization of Time: Temporal Realities and Experience.* Stanford: Stanford University Press.

Boal, Augusto. 1979. *Theater of the Oppressed.* Trans. Center for Inter-American Relations. New York: Urizen Books.

Boquet, Elizabeth. 2002. *Noise from the Writing Center.* Logan: Utah State University Press.

Boyer, Ernest. 1990. *Scholarship Reconsidered: Priorities of the Professoriate.* New York: Jossey-Bass.

Brodkey, Linda. Writing on the Bias. *College English* 56:527–547.

Bruffee, Kenneth. 1984. Peer tutoring and the conversation of mankind. *College English* 46:635–652.

Buckingham, Marcus and Curt Coffman. 1999. *First, Break All the Rules: What the World's Greatest Managers Do Differently.* New York: Simon and Schuster.

Clawson, James and Marcia Conner. 2004. *Creating a Learning Culture: Strategy, Technology, and Practice.* Cambridge: Cambridge University Press.

Conner, Marcia. 2005. Learning Culture Audit. http://www.agelesslearner.com/assess/cultureaudit.html.

Conroy, Thomas Michael, Neal D. Lerner, with Pamela J. Siska. 1998. Graduate Students as WritingTutors: Role Conflict and the Nature of Professionalization. In *Weaving Knowledge Together,* ed. Carol Peterson Haviland, et al. Emmitsburg: NWCA Press.

Davies, Karen. 2001. Responsibility and Daily Life: Reflections Over Timescape. In *Timespace: Geographies of Temporality,* ed. Jon May and Nigel Thrift. London and New York: Routledge.

Day, Kami and Michele Eodice. 2001. *(First Person)2 : A Study of Co-Authoring in the Academy.* Logan: Utah State University Press.

de Certeau, Michel. 1988. *The Practice of Everyday Life,* trans. Steven Rendall. Berkeley: University of California Press.

Doyle, Denise. 2004. The Scholarship of Administration: An Interview with Denise Doyle. *Academic Leader.*

Eodice, Michele. 2003. Breathing Lessons, or Collaboration Is. In Pemberton and Kinkead.

Farrell, Pamela B. [Childers], ed. 1989. *The High School Writing Center: Establishing and Maintaining One.* Urbana: National Council of Teachers of English.

Fontaine, Sheryl I. 2002. Teaching with the Beginner's Mind: Notes from My Karate Journal. *College Composition and Communication* 54:208–221.

Fox, Helen. 1994. *Listening to the World: Cultural Issues in Academic Writing.* Urbana: National Council of Teachers of English.

Frankfurt, Harry G. 2005. *On Bullshit.* New Jersey. Princeton University Press:

Garrison, Roger H. 1995. One-to-One: Tutorial Instruction in Freshman Composition. In *St. Martin's Guide to Teaching Writing. 3rd ed.,* ed. Robert Connors and Cheryl Glenn. New York: St. Martin's Press. (Orig. pub. 1974).

Geller, Anne Ellen. 2005. Tick-Tock, Next: Finding Epochal Time in the Writing Center. *The Writing Center Journal* 25.1.

Gere, Anne Ruggles. 1994. Kitchen tables and rented rooms: The extracurriculum of composition. *College Composition and Communication* 45:75–92.

———. *Writing Groups: History, Theory, and Implications.* Carbondale: Southern Illinois University Press.

Gillespie, Paula and Neal Lerner. 2003. *The Allyn and Bacon Guide to Peer Tutoring, 2nd Edition.* New York: Longman.

Gladwell, Malcolm. 2005. *Blink: The Power of Thinking Without Thinking.* New York: Little, Brown and Company.

Gleick, James. 2000. *Faster: The Acceleration of Just about Everything.* New York: Vintage.

———. 1987. *Chaos: Making a New Science.* New York: Penguin Book.

Glenn, Cheryl. 2004. *Unspoken: A Rhetoric of Silence.* Carbondale: Southern Illinois University Press.

Goldthwaite, Melissa A. 2003. Out of and Back Into the Box: Redefining Essays and Options. *Writing on the Edge* 14:69–88.

Grimm, Nancy Maloney. 1999. *Good Intentions: Writing Center Work for Postmodern Times.* Portsmouth: Boynton/Cook.

Guinier, Lani and Gerald Torres. 2002. *The Miner's Canary: Enlisting Race, Resisting Power, Transforming Democracy.* Cambridge: Harvard University Press.

Harris, Muriel. 1986. *Teaching One-to-One: The Writing Conference.* Urbana: National Council of Teachers of English.

Heidegger, Martin. 1962. *Being and Time.* Trans. John Macquerie and Edward Robinson. San Francisco: Harper.

Hochschild, Arlie. 1997. *The Time Bind: When Work Becomes Home and Home Becomes Work.* New York: Henry Holt.

hooks, bell. 1989. *Talking Back: Thinking Feminist, Thinking Black.* Cambridge: South End Press.

Hyde, Lewis. 1998. *Trickster Makes This World: Mischief, Myth and Art.* New York: Farrar, Straus and Giroux.

———. 1983. *The Gift: Imagination and the Erotic Life of Property.* New York:Random House

Illich, Ivan. 2004. *Deschooling Society.* New York: Marion Boyars. (Orig 1971).

Janangelo, Joseph. 2002. Writing across the curriculum: Contemplating *auteurism* and creativity in writing program direction. In Rose and Weiser.

Jauhar, Sandeep. 2005. Magical Medicine on TV. *New York Times.* July 19.

Kameen, Paul. 2000. *Writing/Teaching: Essays Toward a Rhetoric of Pedagogy.* Pittsburgh: University of Pittsburgh Press.

Kopelson, Karen. 2003. Rhetoric on the Edge of Cunning: Or, The Performance of Neutrality (Re)Considered as a Composition Pedagogy for Student Resistance. *College Composition and Communication* 55:15–146.

Koster, Jo. 2003. Administration Across the Curriculum: or Practicing What We Preach. In Pemberton and Kinkead.

Langer, Ellen. 1997. *The Power of Mindful Learning.* Cambridge MA: Perseus Books.

Lave, Jean and Etienne Wenger. 1991. *Situated Learning: Legitimate Peripheral Participation.* Cambridge: Cambridge University Press.

Lefebvre, Henri. 1992. *Critique of Everyday Life.* Trans. John Moore. New York: Verso.

Levine, Robert. 1997. *The Geography of Time: The Temporal Misadventures of a Social Psychologist, or How Every Culture Keeps Time Just a Little Bit Differently.* New York: Basic Books/HarperCollins.

Lightman, Alan. 1993. *Einstein's Dreams.* New York: Warner Books.

Limerick, Patricia N. 1993. Dancing with Professors: The Trouble with Academic Prose. *New York Times Book Review.* October 31.

Lu, Min-Zhan. 1987. From Silence to Words: Writing as Struggle. *College English* 49:437–448.

McAndrew, Donald and Thomas Reigstad. 2001. *Tutoring Writing: A Practical Guide for Conferences.* Portsmouth: Boynton/Cook.

McIntosh, Peggy. 2005. White Privilege: Unpacking the Invisible Knapsack. In *White Privilege: Essential Readings on the Other Side of Racism,* ed. Paula S. Rothenberg. New York: Worth.

McKinney, Jackie Grutsch. 2005. Leaving Home Sweet Home: Towards Critical Readings of Writing Center Spaces. *The Writing Center Journal* 25.2:6–20.

Meyer, Emily and Louise Smith. 1987. *The Practical Tutor.* New York: Oxford University Press.

Minnesota Collaborative Anti-Racism Initiative. 2005. *Understanding and Dismantling Racism: MCARI Anti-Racism Team Workshop.* Participant Workbook. Minneapolis: MCARI.

The Mirror. Fairfield University campus newspaper. 20.26: 1.

Murphy, Christina and Steve Sherwood. 2003. *The St. Martin's Sourcebook for Writing Tutors.* Boston: Bedford/St. Martin's.

Murray, Donald. 1968. *A Writer Teaches Writing: A Practical Method of Teaching Composition.* Boston: Houghton-Mifflin.

Newkirk, Thomas. 1997. *The Performance of Self in Student Writing.* Portsmouth: Boynton/ Cook.

Newman, Judith. 1987. Learning to Teach by Uncovering Our Assumptions *Language Arts* 64.7:727–737. http://www.lupinworks.com/article/learn.html.

Palmer, Parker. 1998. *The Courage to Teach: Exploring the Inner Landscape of a Teacher's Life.* San Francisco: Jossey-Bass.

Pemberton, Michael A. and Joyce Kinkead eds. 2003. *The Center Will Hold: Critical Perspectives on Writing Center Scholarship.* Logan: Utah State University Press.

Phelps, Louise W. 2002 Turtles all the way down: Educating for academic leadership. In *The Writing Program Administrators' Resource: a Guide to Reflective Institutional Practice.* S. Brown and Teresa Enos Eds. Mahwah: Erlbaum.

Prisoners Of Time, Report of the National Education Commission on Time and Learning. 1994. http://www.ed.gov/pubs/PrisonersOfTime/index.html.

Pryor, Karen. 1999. *Don't Shoot the Dog: The New Art of Teaching and Training.* New York: Bantam.

Rafoth, Ben. 2000. *A Tutor's Guide: Helping Writers One to One.* Portsmouth: Boynton/ Cook.

Ramsey, William. 2005. *Friends of Writing Center Journal Blog.* http://writingcenterjournal. blogspot.com. March 28.

Robinson, John and Geoffrey Godbey. 1999. *Time for Life: The Surprising Ways Americans Use Their Time (Re-Reading the Canon) 2nd ed.* University Park: Pennsylvania State University Press.

Rose, Shirley K. and Irwin Weiser. 2002. *The Writing Program Administrator as Theorist: Making Knowledge Work.* Portsmouth: Boynton/Cook-Heinemann.

Rowe, Mary Budd. 1987. Wait Time: Slowing Down May Be a Way of Speeding Up. *American Educator* 11: 38–43.

Roy, Beth. 2002. For White People, on How to Listen When Race is the Subject. *The Journal of Intergroup Relations.* 29.3:3–15.

Schechner, Richard. 2003. *Performance Theory.* New York: Routledge.

Schön, Donald. 1987. *Educating the Reflective Practitioner: Toward a New Design for Teaching and Learning in the Professions.* San Francisco: Jossey-Bass.

Sirc, Geoffrey. 2002. *English Composition as a Happening.* Logan: Utah State University Press.

Senge, Peter. 1990. *The Fifth Discipline: The Art and Practice of the Learning Organization.* New York: Currency Doubleday.

Senge, Peter, et al. 2000. *Schools That Learn: A Fifth Discipline Fieldbook for Educators, Parents, and Everyone Who Cares About Education.* New York: Currency Doubleday.

Smith, Christopher. 2005. *The Benefits of Speed Golf.* Speed Golf International. http://speed-golfinternational.com/articlebenefits.htm. June 15.

Smith, Erec. 2005. Trickster Pedagogy: A new guiding myth to tutoring. Paper presented at the annual meeting of the Conference on College Composition and Communication, San Francisco.

Solnit, Rebecca. 2004. *A Field Guide to Getting Lost.* New York: Viking Press.

Spellmeyer, Kurt. 1996. After Theory: From Textuality to Attunement With the World. *College English* 58:893–913.

———. 2003. *Arts of Living: Reinventing the Humanities for the Twenty-first Century.* Albany: State University of New York Press.

Stahl, Robert J. 1994. Using Think-time and Wait-time Skillfully in the Classroom. http://atozteacherstuff.com/pages/1884.shtml.

Starratt, Robert J. 1993. The *Drama of Leadership.* London: The Falmer Press.

Stuckey, J. Elspeth. 1991. *The Violence of Literacy.* Portsmouth: Boynton/Cook.

Tagg, John. 2003. *The Learning Paradigm College.* Bolton MA: Anker Press.

Tatum, Beverly. 1997. *Why Are All the Black Kids Sitting Together in the Cafeteria? And Other Conversations about Race.* New York: Basic Books.

Tri-Council Coordinating Committee/Minnesota Collaborative Anti-Racism Initiative. 2005. *Understanding and Dismantling Racism: Anti-Racism Training Manual.* Minneapolis and Chicago: Tri-Council Coordinating Commission and Crossroads.

Weick, Karl. 1979. *The Social Psychology of Organizing.* Reading: Addison-Wesley Publishing Company.

Welch, Nancy. 1997. *Getting Restless: Rethinking Revision in Writing Instruction.* Portsmouth: Heinemann-Boynton/Cook.

Wenger, Etienne. 1998. *Communities of Practice: Learning, Meaning, and Identity.* Cambridge: Cambridge University Press.

———, Richard McDermott, & William M. Snyder. 2002. *Cultivating Communities of Practice: A Guide to Managing Knowledge.* Boston: Harvard Business School Press.

Williams, Terry Tempest. 2004. *The Open Space of Democracy,* Great Barrington, MA: Orion Society.

Yancey, Kathleen Blake. 2004. Made Not Only in Words: Composition in a New Key. *College Composition and Communication.* 56:297–328.

———. 1998. *Reflection in the Writing Classroom.* Logan: Utah State University Press.

INDEX

ABOUT THE AUTHORS

The five authors administer writing centers and academic programs at Clark University, the University of Oklahoma, St. Cloud State University, Rhode Island College, and Fairfield University. They have served as officers in the International Writing Centers Association, the Midwest Writing Centers Association, and the Northeast Writing Centers Association. They are active in the National Conference on Peer Tutoring in Writing. These five have been nominated for or received several outstanding teaching and scholarship awards and teach a variety of writing, writing center theory and practice, and literature classes.

In addition, they have published in a number of journals and edited collections, including *College Composition and Communication, Writing on the Edge, Composition Studies, Issues in Writing, Journal of Faculty Development, The Writing Center Journal, College Teaching, Journal of Teaching in Social Work, Stories from the Center, The Center Will Hold, Writing Groups Inside and Outside the Classroom, Centers for Learning: Writing Centers and Libraries in Collaboration, The Writing Center Resource Manual, Genre Across the Curriculum,* and *Writing Center Research: Extending the Conversation, Creative Approaches to Writing Center Work.* They have written two books, *Noise from the Writing Center* and *(First Person)2: A Study of Co-Authoring in the Academy,* both of which were published by Utah State University Press.